1996

# HIT LIST

## Frequently Challenged Books for

# YOUNG ADULTS

Prepared by
The Intellectual Freedom Committee
of the
Young Adult Library Services Association

*With the Assistance of*
Merri M. Monks
and
Donna Reidy Pistolis

**American Library Association**
Chicago and London
1996

While extensive effort has gone into ensuring the
reliability of information appearing in this book, the
publisher makes no warranty, express or implied, on
the accuracy or reliability of the information, and does
not assume and hereby disclaims any liability to any
person for any loss or damage caused by errors or
omissions in this publication.

Project editor: Louise D. Howe

Cover and text design: Dianne M. Rooney

Composition by Impressions Book and Journal Services, Inc.
in Sabon and Futura using a Penta MV9300

Printed on 50-pound Victor Offset, a pH-neutral stock,
and bound in 10-point C1S cover stock by Victor
Graphics, Inc.

The paper used in this publication meets the minimum
requirements of American National Standards for
Information Sciences—Permanence of Paper for
Printed Library Materials, ANSI Z39.48-1992. ⊚

**Library of Congress Cataloging-in-Publication Data**

Hit list : frequently challenged books for young adults / prepared by
   the Intellectual Freedom Committee of the Young Adult Library
   Services Association, a division of the American Library Association :
   with the assistance of Merri M. Monks and Donna Reidy Pistolis.
        p.   cm.
     ISBN 0-8389-3459-5 (alk. paper)
     1. Challenged books—United States—Bibliography.   2. Children's
   literature, English—Bibliography.   I. Monks, Merri M.
   II. Pistolis, Donna Reidy.   III. Young Adults Library Services
   Association. Intellectual Freedom Committee.
   Z1019.H68   1996
   098'.1'0973—dc20                                              98-14418

Printed in the United States of America.

00  99  98  97  96     5  4  3  2  1

# CONTENTS

INTRODUCTION    *vii*

    *Roger Sutton*


**MARK TWAIN**

    The Adventures of Huckleberry Finn    *1*

**NANCY GARDEN**

    Annie on My Mind    *5*

**RON KOERTGE**

    The Arizona Kid    *8*

**MALCOLM X AND ALEX HALEY**

    The Autobiography of Malcolm X:
    As Told to Alex Haley    *11*

**J. D. SALINGER**

    The Catcher in the Rye    *14*

**ROBERT CORMIER**

    The Chocolate War    *19*

**STEPHEN KING**

    Christine    *24*

**JEAN AUEL**
The Clan of the Cave Bear    27

**ALICE WALKER**
The Color Purple    30

**ROBERT NEWTON PECK**
A Day No Pigs Would Die    35

**WALTER DEAN MYERS**
Fallen Angels    38

**V. C. ANDREWS**
Flowers in the Attic    41

**JUDY BLUME**
Forever    43

**ANONYMOUS**
Go Ask Alice    47

**PAT CONROY**
The Great Santini    51

**JOHN GARDNER**
Grendel    53

**MARGARET ATWOOD**
The Handmaid's Tale    56

**ROBERT CORMIER**
I Am the Cheese    60

**MAYA ANGELOU**
I Know Why the Caged Bird Sings    63

**WILLIAM GOLDING**
Lord of the Flies    67

**JOHN STEINBECK**
Of Mice and Men    72

**S. E. HINTON**
The Outsiders    76

**CHRIS CRUTCHER**
Running Loose    80

**KURT VONNEGUT**
Slaughterhouse-Five; or, The Children's Crusade    82

**LINDA MADARAS WITH DANE SAAVEDRA**
The What's Happening to My Body Book for Boys    86

**LINDA MADARAS WITH DANE SAAVEDRA**
The What's Happening to My Body Book for Girls    86

APPENDIX
What ALA Can Do to Help
Librarians Combat Censorship    89

# INTRODUCTION

**H**it List: *Frequently Challenged Young Adult Titles; References to Defend Them* was first published in 1989 and included annotations, review citations, and other bibliographic backup for twenty young adult titles that have been frequent targets of censorship attempts. This expanded update, prepared by YALSA's Intellectual Freedom Committee and the YALSA office, includes "case files" for twenty-six books, retaining (and updating) ten from the first edition and adding sixteen others that have more recently found themselves subject to attacks and challenges. Huck Finn and Holden Caulfield are now joined by the likes of Chris Crutcher's headstrong Louie Banks, Stephen King's malevolent Christine, and John Gardner's long-suffering Grendel. Sandra Scoppetone's young lovers, Jaret and Peggy (in *Happy Endings Are All Alike*), have found themselves replaced—in the censors' eyes, anyway—by Nancy Garden's Liza and Annie (in *Annie on My Mind*). Garden stood up in a Kansas courtroom in 1995 and emerged victorious.

YALSA hopes that *Hit List* will give librarians who are faced with censorship attempts a place to start. Each entry includes an annotation for the book in question; examples of recent challenges; citations to reviews of the book, background articles, and articles about the book and author; a list of awards and recommended reading where the book is cited; and audiovisual resources. This information can help you prepare a defense when a book is challenged; it can also help you understand *why* a book is being challenged.

It is also important to note that these listings can serve as a model. Perhaps Walter Dean Myers's *Fallen Angels* is not being challenged in your library; instead, someone is asking that his *Scorpions*, for example, be removed from the shelves. Do what is done here: prepare a summary and defense of the book, find out where else it has been challenged and why, and gather reviews and recommendations. YALSA and ALA's Office for Intellectual Freedom can help with this (see the essay "What ALA Can Do to Help Librarians Combat Censorship" found on page 89).

We would like to thank the 1992–1994 YALSA Intellectual Freedom Committee and their chairperson, Patricia Muller, the 1995–1996 YALSA president. We would also like to thank the ALA Office for Intellectual Freedom for their cooperation and support. In addition, we would like to thank Josephine C. Sharif, the AASL/YALSA Coordinator for Publications, for her expert assistance.

Roger Sutton
Editor-in-Chief
*Horn Book Magazine*

# The Adventures of Huckleberry Finn

London: Chatto & Windus, 1884

*The Adventures of Huckleberry Finn* is generally recognized as a comic and biting condemnation of the callousness of a society that pretended to value virtue while condoning slavery. Huck, though crude and unpolished by society's standards, has the moral strength to do what he is convinced is right. He helps the slave Jim escape, even though it means breaking the law, and even if it means going to hell. Huck's kindness and integrity and Jim's generosity and dignity present a striking contrast to the meanness, corruption, and deceit of the so-called "civilized folks" with which they meet as they travel down the Mississippi River.

Most scholars of American literature consider *The Adventures of Huckleberry Finn* to be one of the three or four most-listed masterpieces of American literature. *The Scarlet Letter* and *Moby Dick* are the others most frequently listed. Many authors have praised the novel, including T. S. Eliot and Ernest Hemingway, and have admitted to being influenced by Twain in their own works. Hemingway went so far as to declare that all of contemporary American literature derives from *Huckleberry Finn*.

When *The Adventures of Huckleberry Finn* was first published, it was criticized as being profane and setting a vulgar example for young and impressionable readers. More recently it has been condemned by some black parents and educators as racist and demeaning, adding that the character of Jim presents an embarrassing and negative image of their race to black children. However, both scholars and generations of thoughtful readers have been moved by the story and the decency of Huck and Jim. It is considered by many to be the quintessential depiction of the American character, faithfully delineating both its native virtues and its deepest flaws.

## Challenges

*The Adventures of Huckleberry Finn* was banned in Concord, Massachusetts (1885), as "trash and suitable only for the slums."

The book was excluded from the children's room of the Brooklyn (N.Y.) Public Library (1905) on the grounds that "Huck not only itched but scratched, and that he said 'sweat' when he should have said 'perspiration.' "

It was confiscated at the USSR border in 1930. The book was dropped from the New York City list of approved books for senior and junior high schools (1957), partly because of objections to frequent use of the term *nigger*.

Removed from the Miami Dade (Fla.) Junior College required-reading list (1969) because the book "creates an emotional block for black students that inhibits learning."

*The Adventures of Huckleberry Finn* was challenged as a "racist" novel in Winnetka, Illinois (1976); Warrington, Pennsylvania (1981); Davenport, Iowa (1981); Fairfax County, Virginia (1982); Houston, Texas (1982); State College, (Pa.) Area School District (1983); Springfield, Illinois (1984); and Waukegan, Illinois (1984).

The book was removed from the required-reading list in the Rockford (Ill.) public schools (1988) because the book contains the word *nigger*.

Challenged at the Berrien Springs (Mich.) High School (1988).

Removed from a required-reading list and school libraries in Caddo Parish, Louisiana (1988), because of racially offensive passages.

Challenged at the Sevier County High School in Sevierville, Tennessee (1989), because of racial slurs and dialect.

Challenged on an Erie (Pa.) High School supplemental English reading list (1990) because of its derogatory references to African Americans.

Challenged in the Plano (Tex.) Independent School District (1990) because the novel is "racist."

Challenged in the Mesa (Ariz.) Unified School District (1991) because the book repeatedly uses the word *nigger* and damages the self-esteem of black youth.

Removed from the required-reading list of the Terrebone Parish public schools in Houma, Louisiana (1991), because of the repeated use of the word *nigger*.

Temporarily pulled from the Portage (Mich.) classrooms (1991) after some black parents complained that their children were uncomfortable with the book's portrayal of blacks.

Challenged in the Kinston (N.C.) Middle School (1992) when the superintendent said that the novel could not be assigned because the students were too young to read the book because of its use of the word *nigger*.

Challenged at the Modesto (Calif.) High School as a required reading (1992) because of "offensive and racist language."

Challenged at the Carlisle (Pa.) area schools (1993) because the book's racial slurs are offensive to both black and white students.

Challenged, but retained on high school reading lists by the Lewisville (Tex.) School Board (1994).

Challenged in English classes at Taylor County High School in Butler, Georgia (1994), because it contains racial slurs and bad grammar and does not reject slavery.

Challenged by a parent in Modesto, California (1992), who asked to have it dropped from recommended high school reading lists because of the use of the word *nigger*, a "disparaging and depreciatory term that has no place in our classrooms."

Removed from a mandatory reading list in Houma, Louisiana (1992), after objections that "it was a hardship on a lot of young kids . . . as soon as it got to the word *nigger*, the white students would laugh at them."

## Articles about This Book

Barlow, Dudley. "Why We Still Need Huckleberry Finn." *Education Digest* 58 (Sept. 1992): 31–35.

"Black Writers on Huckleberry Finn." *Mark Twain Journal* 22 (Fall 1984): 1–52 (special issue).

Cloonan, M. V. "Censorship of *The Adventures of Huckleberry Finn*: An Investigation." *Top of the News* 40 (Winter 1984): 189–96.

Nichol, Charles. "One Hundred Years on a Raft: A Dirty Word with the Huck Finn Critics." *Harpers Magazine* 272 (Jan. 1986): 65–68.

## Background

Because Mark Twain is one of the three or four most important figures in American literature, biographical information concerning him, his literary and philosophical aims, and his opinions is available in many sources. The biographies listed below are standard works.

Hill, Hamlin. *Mark Twain: God's Fool*. New York: Harper, 1973.

Kaplan, Justin. *Mark Twain and His World*. New York: Simon & Schuster, 1974.

Kaplan, Justin. *Mr. Clemens and Mark Twain: A Biography*. New York: Simon & Schuster, 1966.

*Satire or Evasion?: Black Perspectives on Huckleberry Finn*. Eds. James S. Leonard, Thomas Asa Tenney, and Thadious M. Davis. Durham, N.C.: Duke University Press, 1992.

Smith, Henry Nash. *Mark Twain: The Development of a Writer*. Cambridge, Mass.: Harvard University Press, 1962.

The following are standard critical analyses of Twain's work.

Blair, Walter. *Mark Twain and Huckleberry Finn*. Berkeley, Calif.: University of California Press, 1960.

Eliot, T. S. "An Introduction to *Huckleberry Finn*." In *Adventures of Huckleberry Finn: An Authoritative Text, Backgrounds and Sources, Criticism*. 2nd ed. Ed. Sculley Bradley and others. New York: Norton, 1977. pp. 328–35.

Hearn, Michael Patrick. *The Annotated Huckleberry Finn*. New York: Potter, 1981.

Kaplan, Justin. *Born to Trouble: One Hundred Years of Huckleberry Finn*. Washington: Library of Congress, 1985.

Kazin, Alfred. *An American Procession*. New York: Knopf, 1984. pp. 181–210.

*One Hundred Years of "Huckleberry Finn": The Boy, His Book, and American Culture*. Eds. Robert Sattelmeyer and J. Donald Crowley. Columbia, Mo.: University of Missouri Press, 1985.

Trilling, Lionel. *The Liberal Imagination*. New York: Harcourt, 1979, pp. 104–17.

## References about the Author

*Twentieth-Century Literary Criticism.* Detroit: Gale, 1982. v. 6, pp. 452–88; v. 12, pp. 423–55; v. 19, pp. 349–417. The entry in v. 19 is devoted exclusively to excerpts from critical essays and analyses of *The Adventures of Huckleberry Finn.*

*Yesterday's Authors of Books for Children.* Ed. Anne Commire. Detroit: Gale, 1978. v. 2, pp. 50–83.

## Sources Recommending This Book

Suggested reading lists for secondary students, almost without exception, list *The Adventures of Huckleberry Finn* as a work of literature that all students should have read by the time they complete high school. The following are some examples of those many lists of recommended reading on which the novel appears.

*Fiction Catalog,* 13th ed. Eds. Juliette Yaakov and Jack Greenfieldt. New York: H. W. Wilson, 1996. p. 658.

Gillespie, John T., ed. *Best Books for Junior High Readers.* New Providence, N.J.: R. R. Bowker, 1991. p. 18.

Gillespie, John T., ed. *Best Books for Senior High Readers.* New Providence, N.J.: R. R. Bowker, 1991. p. 23.

*Growing Up Is Hard to Do.* Ed. Sally Estes. Chicago: Booklist/American Library Association, 1994. pp. 19, 28.

*Junior High School Library Catalog,* Ed. Juliette Yaakov. 6th ed. New York: H. W. Wilson, 1990. p. 418.

*Senior High School Library Catalog.* 14th ed. New York: H. W. Wilson, 1992. p. 724.

Young Adult Library Services Association. *Outstanding Books for the College Bound: Choices for a Generation.* Chicago: American Library Association, 1996.

*The Young Adult Reader's Adviser.* Vol. 1, *The Best in Literature and Language Arts, Mathematics, and Computer Science.* Ed. Myra Immell. New Providence, N.J.: R. R. Bowker, 1992. v. 1, pp. 181–82.

## Audiovisual Resources

*The Adventures of Huckleberry Finn.* 1/2-inch videocassette (VHS). 89 min. Producer and distributor: Guidance Associates, 90 South Bedford Rd., Mt. Kisco, NY 10549; (800) 431-1242, (914) 666-4100, fax: (914) 666-5319.

NANCY GARDEN

# Annie on My Mind

New York: Farrar, Straus, Giroux, 1982

Liza, now in college, ponders her relationship with Annie, whom she met when she was 17 while visiting the Metropolitan Museum of Art. As the two discover that they have mutual interests, likes, and dislikes, friendship blossoms into love. In lyrical terms, rather than graphic description, Liza recounts the consummation of their love during a house-sitting at her teacher's home. Her confusion over her sexuality and her desire to hide from her family and friends that which is becoming evident to her is reflected in her withdrawal from all contacts except those with Annie.

Annie is destined for Berkeley, while Liza is going to MIT; and their parting is fraught with uncertainty as to their future together. The uncertainty arises from family pressures and from the unpleasant hearing that ensues after Liza and Annie are discovered making love at the home of two teachers who are lesbians, and who have successfully hidden their relationship for many years. The portrayal of these two women, although older, who have lived through the same experience is a bit too coincidental; but it does point out the changing attitudes that will come. The vituperative headmistress who brings charges against the two teachers for encouraging "sexual misbehavior" is herself discharged for her attacks against them and for illegally discharging the teachers. They in turn accept dismissal, as they have in the past when their relationship has come to light.

At the close of the book, Liza has come to accept her own sexuality and phones Annie to tell her that they will be together during Christmas break.

## Challenges

Challenged at the Cedar Mill Community Library in Portland, Oregon, in 1988 because the book portrays lesbian love and sex as normal. Challenged in the Colony, Texas, Public Library in 1992 because "it promotes and encourages the gay lifestyle."

Challenged because it "encourages and condones" homosexuality, but retained at the Bend, Oregon, High School in 1993.

Challenged, but retained at the Lapper, Michigan, West High School Library in 1993.

Challenged at several Kansas City area schools in 1993 after the books were donated by a national group that seeks to give young adults "fair, accurate, and inclusive images of lesbians and gay men"—at the Shawnee Mission School District the book was returned to general circulation; at the Olathe East High School the book was removed; protesters burned copies of the book, but the Kansas City, Missouri, School District kept Garden's novel on the high-school shelves; in Kansas City, Kansas, the school district donated the book to the city's public library; and in Lee's Summitt, the superintendent removed the book.

Challenged, but retained at the Liberty, Missouri, High School Library in 1994.

Removed in 1994 from the Chanute, Kansas, High School library shelves and access limited to those with written parental permission because of concerns about the content.

In 1995, U.S. District Court Judge Thomas Van Bebber ruled that the Olathe School District violated the First Amendment when it removed the book from library shelves; the judge called the action "viewpoint discrimination," and he said that the removal violated Olathe students' and teachers' right to free access to information. In his order Van Bebber wrote, "Although local school boards have broad discretion in the management of school affairs, they must act within fundamental constitutional limits."

## Reviews

*Booklist* 78 (Aug. 1982): 1517; 87 (Sept. 1, 1990): 39; 91 (Oct. 15, 1994): 413.

*Book Report* 11 (March 1993): 65.

*Bulletin of the Center for Children's Books* 36 (Dec. 1982): 66.

*Children's Book Review Service* 11 (Oct. 1982): 18.

*Commonweal* 111 (March 23, 1984): 176.

*English Journal* 73 (Nov. 1984): 61.

*Interracial Books for Children Bulletin* 14 (Jan. 1983): 35.

*Journal of Reading* 26 (Feb. 1983): 468.

*Kirkus Reviews* 50 (June 1, 1982): 637.

*Kliatt Young Adult Paperback Book Guide* 18 (Fall 1984): 8; 26 (Nov. 1992): 4.

*Ms.* 3 (Jan. 1993): 62.

*Publishers Weekly* 222 (Sept. 10, 1982): 75; 239 (Sept. 14, 1992): 127.

*School Librarian* 37 (Aug. 1989): 114.

*School Library Journal* 28 (Aug. 1982): 125; 41 (Feb. 1995): 33.

*Voice of Youth Advocates* 5 (Aug. 1982): 30; 15 (Dec. 1992): 320.

## Background

Cuseo, Allan. *Homosexual Characters in YA Novels: A Literary Analysis 1969–1982.* Metuchen, N.J.: Scarecrow, 1992.

## Awards and Prizes

Best Books for Young Adults, 1982

Best of the Best Books for Young Adults, 1983

Here We Go Again: 25 Years of Best Books, 1994

Nothin' But the Best Books for Young Adults, 1988

"Reviewer's Choice, 1982," *Booklist* (Jan. 15, 1983): 671

## References about the Author

*Contemporary Authors, New Revision Series.* Detroit: Gale, 1990. v. 30.

*Something about the Author, Autobiography Series.* Detroit: Gale, 1989. v. 8.

Ward, Martha E., and others. *Authors of Books for Young People.* 3rd ed. Metuchen, N.J.: Scarecrow, 1990.

## Sources Recommending This Book

Carter, Betty. *Best Books for Young Adults: The History, the Selections, the Romance.* Chicago: American Library Association, 1994. pp. 100, 163, 174, 175.

Gillespie, John T., ed. *Best Books for Junior High Readers.* New Providence, N.J.: R. R. Bowker, 1991. p. 37.

*Growing Up Is Hard to Do.* Ed. Sally Estes. Chicago: Booklist/American Library Association, 1994. pp. 7, 31.

*Juniorplots 4: A Book Talk Guide for Use with Readers Ages 12–16.* Eds. John T. Gillespie and Corrine J. Nader. New York: R. R. Bowker, 1993. p. 61.

Kaywell, Joan F. *Adolescents at Risk: A Guide to Fiction and Nonfiction for Young Adults, Parents, and Professionals.* Westport, Conn.: Greenwood, 1993. p. 38.

*Senior High School Library Catalog.* 14th ed. Eds. Brenda Smith and Juliette Yaakov. New York: H. W. Wilson, 1992. p. 686.

Spencer, Pam. *What Do Young Adults Read Next? A Reader's Guide to Fiction for Young Adults.* Detroit: Gale, 1994. pp. 171, 189.

*Top One Hundred Countdown: Best of the Best Books for Young Adults, 1969–1994.* Chicago: American Library Association, 1995.

Zvirin, Stephanie. *The Best Years of Their Lives: A Resource Guide for Teenagers in Crisis.* 2nd ed. Chicago: American Library Association, 1996. p. 89.

# The Arizona Kid

Boston: Joy Street Books, 1988

A boy's "sweet sixteen" novel, *The Arizona Kid* recounts one summer in the life of Billy, a short guy from Bradley-ville, Missouri, who visits his gay Uncle Wes in Tucson for the summer. Wes gets Billy a job at a racetrack. He meets Cara Mae at work, falls in love with her, and has his first sexual relationship with her.

He also gets to know his uncle better and learns about the problems Wes faces as a gay man in a homophobic world.

When Wes sees Billy's obvious infatuation with Cara, he teaches Billy about safe sex—not just the mechanics of carrying and using condoms, but the importance of protecting himself, his current girlfriend, and any future partners he may have from possible exposure to HIV. Wes also teaches Billy about love and tolerance.

Billy isn't entirely comfortable with Wes's sexual orientation at the beginning of the summer, nor is he completely comfortable with it by summer's end. But he comes to love and value his uncle and to see the unfairness of the prejudice to which Wes and his friends are subjected. He also begins to see the devastation AIDS has wreaked in the lives of some of Wes's friends.

Other thematic threads in the story include Billy's friendships with his track co-worker, Lew, and Lew's sexy girlfriend, Abby. Lew, Abby, Billy, and Cara Mae sometimes spend evenings together, drinking beer, smoking pot, and driving around the desert. Lew often tries to persuade Billy to reveal the intimate details of his relationship with Cara Mae, the results of which are generally quite humorous. Additionally, the unpredictable physiological problems a young man can face—erections at times that embarrass him, the inability to have an erection when he really wants one—are worked meaningfully into the plot, reassuring young male readers that they are not alone in these experiences.

This novel is funny, sexy, and bittersweet; and as Billy's summer comes to an end, he must say good-bye to two people whom he has come to love—Cara Mae and his Uncle Wes. He grows up over the summer, and not just through the important milestone of his first sexual relationship. He experiences a sense of self-worth and self-assurance arising from meaningful work and a loving relationship, and he has developed a stronger sense of himself over this special sixteenth summer.

## Challenges

Because the book "encourages and condones" homosexuality, it was challenged, but retained at the Bend (Oreg.) High School (1993).

After a parent found the content of the book inappropriate for 12- and 13-year-olds, the book was pulled from and later restored to the seventh-grade English classroom at Minnetonka (Minn.) Middle School West (1994).

## Reviews

*Advocate* (July 31, 1990): 71.

*Booklist* 84 (May 1, 1988): 1511; 87 (Sept. 1, 1990): 40; 88 (Nov. 15, 1991): 632; 88 (Jan. 15, 1992): 933; 90 (April 1, 1994): 1463; 91 (Oct. 15, 1994): 415.

*Book Report* 7 (Sept. 1988): 34; 14 (May 1995): 27.

*Bulletin of the Center for Children's Books* 41 (June 1988): 209.

*Children's Book Review Service* 16 (Spring 1988): 134.

*Emergency Librarian* 17 (March 1990): 62.

*Kirkus Reviews* 56 (May 1, 1988): 694.

*New York Times Book Review* 93 (Aug. 1988): 25.

*Publishers Weekly* 233 (May 13, 1988): 278.

*School Librarian* 37 (Nov. 1989): 160.

*School Library Journal* 34 (June 1988): 118; 36 (Nov. 1990): 50; 39 (May 1993): 22; 41 (Feb. 1995): 33.

*Voice of Youth Advocates* 11 (Oct. 1988): 182; 13 (April 1990): 69; 13 (Aug. 1990): 150; 11 (Oct. 1988): 182.

*Wilson Library Bulletin* 63 (April 1989): 97.

## Articles about This Book

Jenkins, Christine. "Being Gay: Gay/Lesbian Characters and Concerns in Young Adult Books." *Booklist* 87 (Sept. 1, 1990): 39–41.

Rochman, Hazel, and Stephanie Zvirin. "Growing Up Male: Boys in Love." *Booklist* 89 (Jan. 15, 1992): 932–33.

Spencer, Pam. "Easy Talking: Humor." *Voice of Youth Advocates* 13 (Aug. 1990): 149–50.

Tait, Sue, and Christy Tyson. "Paperbacks for Young Adults." *Emergency Librarian* 17 (March–April 1990): 61–62.

Tillapaugh, Meg. "AIDS: A Problem for Today's YA Problem Novel." *School Library Journal* 39 (May 1993): 22–25.

## References about the Author

*Something about the Author,* Detroit: Gale, 1988. v. 53, pp. 95–96.

## Sources Recommending This Book

*Best in Children's Books, 1985–90.* Eds. Zena Sutherland, Betsy Hearne, and Roger Sutton. Chicago: University of Chicago Press, 1991. pp. 223–24.

Carter, Betty. *Best Books for Young Adults: The History, the Selections, the Romance.* Chicago: American Library Association, 1994. pp. 115, 168.

*Growing Up Is Hard to Do.* Ed. Sally Estes. Chicago: Booklist/American Library Association, 1994. pp. 22, 32, 56.

*Juniorplots 4: A Book Talk Guide for Use with Readers Ages 12–16.* Eds. John T. Gillespie and Corrine J. Nader. New York: R. R. Bowker, 1993. p. 57.

Rochman, Hazel. *Against Borders: Promoting Books for a Multicultural World.* Chicago: Booklist/American Library Association, 1993. p. 101.

Spencer, Pam. *What Do Young Adults Read Next? A Reader's Guide to Fiction for Young Adults.* Detroit: Gale, 1994. pp. 85, 165, 232, 287, 288, 425, 474, 558.

Zvirin, Stephanie. *The Best Years of Their Lives: A Resource Guide for Teenagers in Crisis.* 2nd ed. Chicago: American Library Association, 1996. p. 89.

# The Autobiography of Malcolm X: As Told to Alex Haley

New York: Grove Press, 1965

The reawakened interest in Malcolm X among young adults—perhaps sparked by Spike Lee's movie, *X*, about the charismatic Muslim leader—has prompted new challenges to this book.

Born in Omaha, Nebraska, in 1925, Malcolm Little was the son of a Baptist preacher. After his father was murdered, his mother's mental health deteriorated, and she was committed to a hospital, leaving Malcolm and his five siblings to be raised in foster homes. Through a connection with an older half-sister, Malcolm eventually made his way to Harlem. There, during World War II, he found his way into Harlem's underworld. Starting as a small-time drug dealer and numbers runner, Malcolm's reputation in the hustlers' world grew. Addicted to drugs and alcohol, he was eventually imprisoned; behind bars, he educated himself, reading voraciously late into the night, his pages illuminated by the dim light of the prison hallway. His reading included the philosophies of Elijah Muhammed, leader of the Nation of Islam. Malcolm converted to the Nation of Islam faith, dropping the name of Little and replacing it with the letter *X*. After his release from prison, Malcolm X became a powerful leader within the Nation's movement. He espoused the Nation's beliefs that blacks should separate themselves from whites and that whites were "devils" who had brainwashed black men.

Malcolm X began to study traditional Middle Eastern Islamic religious tenets and made a *hajj*, or pilgrimage, to the Islamic holy city of Mecca. This, along with other experiences described in his book, caused a series of disagreements between Malcolm X and Elijah Muhammed. When Malcolm broke away from the Nation of Islam to establish a more secular movement based in social change and a belief in the brotherhood of man, and to pursue a traditional Islamic interpretation of his religious faith, he was ostracized by the Nation of Islam. He was assassinated on February 21, 1965.

*The Autobiography of Malcolm X* is regarded by some critics as a great American biographical work. It is a detailed portrait of one brilliant man who suffered the destruction of his family and the lifelong degradation of racial prejudice, who was a criminal and a drug addict, and whose life was altered not just by one, but by two religious conversions.

*The Autobiography of Malcolm X* arouses controversy over its descriptions of sexual relationships, drug and alcohol abuse, and its portrayal of an African American man who openly vocalized his hatred of whites.

## Challenges

Because the slain Muslim leader advocated antiwhite racism and violence, the book was challenged in the Duval County (Fla.) public schools in 1993.

The book was restricted at the Jacksonville (Fla.) middle-school libraries (1994) because it presents a racist view of white people and is a "how-to manual for crime."

## Reviews

*Black American Literature Forum* 24 (Summer 1990): 377.

*Black Scholar* 12 (March 1981): 86; 22 (Fall 1992): 69.

*Booklist* 66 (Jan. 1, 1966): 423; 86 (Jan. 15, 1990): 979.

*Choice* 2 (Jan. 1966): 764; 16 (Dec. 1979): 1274; 16 (Feb. 1980): 1549; 20 (June 1983): 1422; 21 (April 1984): 1102; 25 (April 1988): 1212.

*Christian Century* 92 (May 14, 1975): 500.

*Library Journal* 117 (Oct. 15, 1992): 88.

*Publishers Weekly* 239 (Jan. 13, 1992): 53.

*Social Education* 33 (April 1969): 489.

*Time* 95 (Feb. 23, 1970): 88.

## Awards and Prizes

Anisfield-Wolf Award for best books concerned with racial problems in the field of creative literature, 1965

Still Alive: Best of the Best Books for Young Adults, 1975

## References about the Author

### For Malcolm X

*Contemporary Black Biography.* Vol. 1. Detroit: Gale, 1992.

### For Alex Haley

*Benet's Reader's Encyclopedia.* 3rd ed. New York: Harper, 1987.

*Benet's Reader's Encyclopedia of American Literature.* 1st ed. Eds. George Perkins, Barbara Perkins, and Phillip Leininger. New York: HarperCollins, 1991.

*World Authors, 1975–1980.* Ed. Vineta Colby. New York: Wilson, 1985.

## Sources Recommending This Book

Carter, Betty. *Best Books for Young Adults: The History, the Selections, the Romance.* Chicago: American Library Association, 1994. p. 174.

Gillespie, John T., ed. *Best Books for Senior High Readers.* New Providence, N.J.: R. R. Bowker, 1991. p. 388.

*Growing Up Is Hard to Do.* Ed. Sally Estes. Chicago: Booklist/American Library Association, 1994. p. 40.

*Juniorplots 3: A Book Talk Guide for Use with Readers Ages 12–16.* Eds. John T. Gillespie and Corrine J. Nader. New York: R. R. Bowker, 1987.

Rochman, Hazel. *Against Borders: Promoting Books for a Multicultural World.* Chicago: Booklist/ American Library Association, 1993. pp. 130, 170.

Young Adult Library Services Association. *Outstanding Books for the College Bound: Choices for a Generation.* Chicago: American Library Association, 1996.

*The Young Adult Reader's Adviser.* Vol. 1, *The Best in Literature and Language Arts, Mathematics, and Computer Science.* Ed. Myra Immell. New Providence, N.J.: R. R. Bowker, 1992. v. 1, p. 450. Vol. 2, *The Best in Social Sciences, History, Science, and Health.* New Providence, N.J.: R. R. Bowker, 1992. v. 2, pp. 250–51.

## Audiovisual Resources

*X.* Motion picture. Warner Bros. Pictures, 1992.

# The Catcher in the Rye

Boston: Little, Brown, 1951

It is interesting and ironic that Salinger's *The Catcher in the Rye* is considered both a major work, even a benchmark of postwar American literature, and the progenitor or prototype of the contemporary "young adult problem" novel. Its impact on the literary world of the nineteen fifties and nineteen sixties was nothing short of phenomenal. Salinger was hailed as one of the first of those angry voices that rallied against the smug self-satisfaction of the postwar boom years, when middle-class America perceived itself as the navel of the world.

The novel was controversial from the start, and remains so today. The cause of the complaints has never changed; the book is condemned for the "bad grammar" and "vulgar language" of its protagonist and narrator, Holden Caulfield, a 17-year-old prep-school dropout, and for Holden's preoccupation (some would say obsession) with death and sex.

But these aspects of the book are not cynical attempts to titillate or shock, but deliberate patterns that reveal the purpose or theme of the novel. And Salinger's theme is neither new nor revolutionary. He deals with the difficulty of growing up and achieving a sense of self-worth in a cold and uncaring world that is pre-occupied with the appearances rather than the realities of life. Holden's story is an example of the literary tradition of the "rite of passage" story—the lonely and arduous journey from childhood innocence to adult experience and responsibility.

We meet Holden at just that uncomfortable point of exposure when he is hanging undecided, unprotected, without defenses and so vulnerable, halfway between childhood and adulthood. The difficulty for Holden is that he sees children as dealing directly and clearly with the realities of life, while adults and those who emulate adults are content to deal with appearances. His dilemma is how he can preserve the clear eyes and honesty of childhood as he moves inexorably toward the experiences of adulthood.

This way of perceiving the rite of passage is nothing new, but Salinger breaks with traditional literary format by structuring his story, not in a linear manner, but in both a circle and spiral. Holden advances not by moving forward from one experience to the next, but by going round and round, examining and reinventing his experiences. Such subjectivity in narrative structure and purpose is one of the hallmarks of modern literary technique.

Salinger chooses his words quite

deliberately to distinguish between the formal, genteel, and empty appearances of the "phony" adult world, and the confusing, conflicting impulses of Holden's reality. Holden's language is honest in expressing this confusion and conflict. If *vulgarity* is defined as that which makes people uncomfortable with themselves, then Holden's so-called vulgar language reveals just how uncomfortable we are with his honesty, how unprepared we are to deal with his pain.

## Challenges

Because the book contains profanity, it was banned from the classrooms in the Boron (Calif.) High School in 1989.

Challenged at the Grayslake (Ill.) Community High School in 1991.

Challenged in 1992 at the Jamaica (Sidell, N.Y.) High School because the book contains profanities and depicts premarital sex, alcohol abuse, and prostitution.

In 1992, challenged in Waterloo (Iowa) schools and Duval County (Fla.) public school libraries because of profanity, lurid passages about sex, and statements defamatory to minorities, God, women, and the disabled.

Challenged in 1992 at the Cumberland Valley (Carlisle, Pa.) High School because of a parent's objections that it contains profanity and is immoral.

Challenged but retained at the New Richmond (Wis.) High School, in 1994, for use in some English classes.

Challenged as required reading in the Corona-Norco (Calif.) Unified School District (1993) because it is "centered around negative activity." The book was retained and teachers select alternatives if students object to Salinger's novel.

Challenged as mandatory reading in the Goffstown (N.H.) schools (1994) because of the vulgar words used and the sexual exploits experienced in the book.

## Reviews

*Atlantic* 188 (Aug. 1951): 82.

*Booklist* 91 (June 1, 1995): 1761; 47 (July 15, 1951): 401.

*Catholic World* 174 (Nov. 1951): 154.

*Chicago Tribune,* July 15, 1951, p. 3.

*Choice* 31 (Oct. 1993): 292.

*Christian Science Monitor* 43 (July 19, 1951): 7.

*English Journal* 81 (April 1992): 87; 82 (April 1993): 88.

*Kirkus Reviews* 19 (May 15, 1951): 247.

*Library Journal* 76 (July 1951): 1125.

*Nation* 173 (Sept. 1, 1951): 176.

*New Republic* 125 (July 16, 1951): 20.

*New York Herald Tribune Book Review,* July 15, 1951, p. 3.

*New York Times,* July 15, 1951, p. 5.

*New Yorker* 27 (Aug. 11, 1951): 71.

*Newsweek* 38 (July 16, 1951): 89.

*San Francisco Chronicle,* July 15, 1951, p. 17.

*Saturday Review* 34 (July 14, 1951): 12.

*Time* 58 (July 16, 1951): 96.

*Times Literary Supplement,* Sept. 7, 1951, p. 561.

*Voice of Youth Advocates* 16 (Feb. 1994): 410.

## Articles about This Book

Barr, Donald. "Should Holden Caulfield Read These Books?" *New York Times Book Review* 91 (May 4, 1986): 1+, 50–51.

Bryan, James E. "The Psychological Structure of *The Catcher in the Rye.*" *PMLA* 89 (Oct. 1974): 1064–74.

Coles, Robert. "Reconsideration: J. D. Salinger." *New Republic* 168 (April 28, 1973): 30–32.

Costello, Donald P. "The Language of *The Catcher in the Rye.*" *American Speech* 34 (Oct. 1959): 172–81.

De Luca, Geraldine. "Unself-Conscious Voices: Larger Contexts for Adolescents." *The Lion and the Unicorn* 2 (Fall 1978): 89–108.

Glasser, William. "*The Catcher in the Rye.*" *Michigan Quarterly Review* 15 (Fall 1976): 432–55.

Kaplan, Charles. "Holden and Huck: The Odyssey of Youth." *College English* 28 (Nov. 1956): 76–80.

Kazin, Alfred. "J. D. Salinger: Everybody's Favorite." Atlantic 208 (Aug. 1961): 27–31.

Moss, A. "Catcher Comes of Age." *Esquire* 96 (Dec. 1981): 56–58+.

Ohmann, Carol, and Richard Ohmann. "Reviews, Critics, and *The Catcher in the Rye.*" *Critical Inquiry* 3 (Fall 1976): 15–38.

Pinsker, S. "*The Catcher in the Rye* and All: Is the Age of Formative Books Over?" *Georgia Review* 40 (Winter 1986): 953–67.

Slabey, Robert M. "*The Catcher in the Rye*: Christian Theme and Symbol." *College Language Association Journal* 6 (March 1963): 170–83.

"Special Number: Salinger." *Wisconsin Studies in Contemporary Literature* 4 (Winter 1963): 1–160.

Strauch, Carl F. "King in the Back Row: Meaning through Structure—A Reading of Salinger's *The Catcher in the Rye.*" *Wisconsin Studies in Contemporary Literature* 2 (Winter 1961): 5–30.

Teachout, T. "Salinger Then and Now." *Commentary* 84 (Sept. 1987): 61–64.

## Background

Baumbach, Jonathan. "The Saint as a Young Man: *The Catcher in the Rye* by J. D. Salinger." In *The Landscape of Nightmare; Studies in the Contemporary American Novel.* New York: New York University Press, 1965. pp. 57–67.

Dessner, L. J. "The Salinger Story; or, Have It Your Way." In *Seasoned Authors for a New Season: The Search for Standards in Popular Writing.* 2 vols. Edited by Louis Filler. Bowling Green, Ohio: Bowling Green University Popular Press, 1980. v. 2, pp. 91–97.

French, Warren. *J. D. Salinger.* 2nd rev. ed. Twayne's U.S. Author Series. Boston: G. K. Hall, 1976.

Gwynn, Frederick L., and Joseph Blotner. *The Fiction of J. D. Salinger.* Pittsburgh, Pa.: University of Pittsburgh Press, 1958.

Hamilton, Ian. *J. D. Salinger: A Writing Life.* London: Heinemann; New York: Random House, 1986.

Harper Jr., Howard M. *Desperate Faith; A Study of Bellow, Salinger, Mailer, Baldwin and Updike.* Chapel Hill, N.C.: University of North Carolina Press, 1967. pp. 65–95.

Hassan, Ihab H. "J. D. Salinger: The Quixotic Gesture." In *Radical Innocence; Studies in the Contemporary American Novel.* Princeton, N.J.: Princeton University Press, 1961. pp. 259–89.

Howe, Irving. "The Salinger Cult." In *Celebrations and Attacks: Thirty Years of Literary and Cultural Commentary.* New York: Horizon, 1979. pp. 93–96.

*J. D. Salinger.* Ed. Harold Bloom. New York: Chelsea House, 1987.

Lundquist, James. *J. D. Salinger.* New York: Frederick Ungar, 1978.

Rees, R. "The Salinger Situation." In *Contemporary American Novelists.* Ed. Harry Thornton Moore. Carbondale, Ill.: Southern Illinois University Press, 1964. pp. 95–105.

Riggan, William. "The Naif." In *Picaros, Madmen, Naifs, and Clowns: The Unreliable First-Person Narrator.* Norman, Okla.: University of Oklahoma Press, 1981. pp. 144–70.

*Salinger; A Critical and Personal Portrait.* Ed. Henry A. Grunwald. New York: Harper, 1962.

*Salinger's* Catcher in the Rye: *Clamor vs. Criticism.* Eds. Harold P. Simonson and Philip E. Hager. Boston: D. C. Heath, 1963.

*Studies in J. D. Salinger: Reviews, Essays, and Critiques of* The Catcher in the Rye *and Other Fiction.* Ed. Marvin Laser and Norman Freeman. New York: Odyssey, 1963.

Weinberg, Helen. "J. D. Salinger's Holden and Seymour and the Spiritual Activist Hero." In *The New Novel in America: The Katkan Mode in Contemporary Fiction.* Ithaca, N.Y.: Cornell University Press, 1970. pp. 141–64.

## References about the Author

*Authors and Artists for Young Adults.* Vol. 2. Detroit: Gale, 1989.

*Benet's Reader's Encyclopedia.* 3rd ed. New York: Harper, 1987.

*Contemporary Literary Criticism.* Vol. 56. Detroit: Gale, 1989.

*Something about the Author.* Vol. 67. Detroit: Gale, 1992.

## Sources Recommending This Book

*Fiction Catalog,* 13th ed. Ed. Juliette Yaakov and John Greenfieldt. New York: H. W. Wilson, 1996. p. 572.

*Fiction for Youth: A Guide to Recommended Books.* 2nd ed. Ed. Lilian Shapiro. New York: Neal-Schuman Publishers, 1986. pp. 164–65.

Gillespie, John T., ed. *Best Books for Senior High Readers.* New Providence, N.J.: R. R. Bowker, 1991. p. 74.

*Junior High School Library Catalog.* 6th ed. Ed. Juliette Yaakov. New York: H. W. Wilson, 1990. p. 410.

Kaywell, Joan F. *Adolescents at Risk: A Guide to Fiction and Nonfiction for Young Adults, Parents and Professionals.* Westport, Conn.: Greenwood, 1993. p. 9.

*The Reader's Advisor: The Best in Reference Works, British Literature & American Literature.* 14th ed. 3 vols. New York: R. R. Bowker, 1994. v. 1, pp. 1042–43.

*Senior High School Library Catalog.* 14th ed. Eds. Brenda Smith and Juliette Yaakov. New York: H. W. Wilson, 1992. p. 716.

Young Adult Library Services Association. *Outstanding Books for the College Bound: Choices for a Generation.* Chicago: American Library Association, 1996.

*The Young Adult Reader's Adviser.* Vol. 1, *The Best in Literature and Language Arts, Mathematics, and Computer Science.* Ed. Myra Immell. New Providence, N.J.: R. R. Bowker, 1992. pp. 282–83.

## Audiovisual Resources

*The Catcher in the Rye.* 3/4- or 1/2-inch videocassette, color. In "Man's Search for Identity." Producer: Center for Humanities, Communications Park, Box 1000, Mt. Kisco, NY 10549–0101. Distributor: Guidance Associates, 90 South Bedford Road, Mt. Kisco, NY 10549; (800) 431-1242.

# The Chocolate War

New York: Pantheon Books, 1974

When Jerry Renault refuses to partici-pate in the chocolate sale at his Catho-lic prep school, Trinity High, he be-comes a hero to his schoolmates. But his refusal is a challenge that Brother Leon and the Vigils, the school's secret society, cannot abide. Slowly, support for Renault falls away, and with the blessings of Brother Leon, Jerry is abandoned to the brutal revenge of the Vigils.

The Chocolate War has been criticized and challenged for its pessi-mism, harsh portrayal of adults and adult authority, and merciless picture of school life. It has been praised by reviewers and critics for its realism, lit-erary style, and its underlying assump-tion that young adult readers are capa-ble of critical thinking and able to form reasoned opinions about the world they inhabit. Cormier has been lauded for his use of language and symbolism. The New York Times has placed this novel on a par with Gold-ing's Lord of the Flies and Knowles's A Separate Peace. Part of the novel's appeal to teen readers is its brutally honest picture of school life.

The novel's careful construction, terse readability, and ability to pro-voke discussion have resulted in its be-ing a recommended addition to many high school English curricula. The

Chocolate War appears on many sug-gested-reading lists and is recognized as a young adult novel that respects the intelligence of its readers by offer-ing them more than a happy ending and a simplistic solution.

## Challenges

Challenged and temporarily removed from the English curriculum in two Lapeer, Michigan, high schools (1981) because of "offensive language and ex-plicit descriptions of sexual situations in the book."

Removed from the Liberty High School in Westminster, Maryland (1982), due to the book's "foul lan-guage" and its portrayal of violence and degradation of schools and teachers.

Challenged at the Richmond, Rhode Island, High School (1983) be-cause the book was deemed "porno-graphic" and "repulsive."

Banned from the Richland Two School District middle-school libraries in Columbia, South Carolina (1984), due to "language problems" but later reinstated for eighth-graders only.

Removed from the Lake Havasu, Arizona, High School freshman read-ing list (1984). The school district board charged the Havasu teachers with failing to set good examples for students, fostering disrespect in the classroom, and failing to support the board.

Challenged at the Cornwall (N.Y.) High School (1985) because the novel is "humanistic and destructive of religious and moral beliefs and of national spirit."

Banned from the Stroudsburg (Pa.) High School Library (1985) because it is "blatantly graphic, pornographic, and wholly unacceptable for a high school library."

Challenged at Barnstable High School in Hyannis, Massachusetts (1986), because of the novel's "profanity, eleven obscene references to masturbation and sexual fantasies," and "ultimately because of the pessimistic ending." The novel, complainants said, fostered negative impressions of authority, of school systems, and of religious schools.

Challenged in the Bay County's four middle schools and three high schools in Panama City, Florida (1986), because it contains "profanity and sexually explicit passages."

Challenged at the Moreno Valley (Calif.) High School Library as "obscene, profane, and sexually explicit."

Suspended from classroom use, pending review, at the Woodsville High School in Haverhill, New Hampshire (1990), because the novel contains expletives, references to masturbation and sexual fantasies, and derogatory characterizations of teachers and of religious ceremonies.

Challenged as suitable curriculum material in the Harwinton and Burlington (Conn.) schools (1990) because it contains profanity and subject matter that sets bad examples and gives students negative views of life.

Challenged at the New Milford (Conn.) schools (1992) because the novel contains language, sexual references, violence, subjectivity, and negativism that are harmful to students.

Challenged at the Kyrene (Ariz.) elementary schools (1993) because of a masturbation scene.

Returned to the Hephzibah High School tenth-grade reading list in Augusta, Georgia (1994), after the complainant said, "I don't see anything educational about that book. If they ever send a book like that home with one of my daughters again, I will personally burn it and throw the ashes on the principal's desk."

Challenged as required reading in the Hudson Falls (N.Y.) schools (1994) because the book has a recurring theme of rape, masturbation, violence, and degrading treatment of women.

## Reviews

*America* 130 (May 4, 1974): 350.

*American Libraries* 5 (Oct. 1974): 492.

*Booklist* 71 (March 15, 1975): 747; 80 (Oct. 15, 1983): 352; 85 (May 1, 1989): 1541; 91 (June 1, 1995): 1760.

*Bulletin of the Center for Children's Books* 27 (July 1974): 173.

*Choice* 12 (Nov. 1975): 1132.

*English Journal* 62 (Jan. 1975): 112; 82 (April 1993): 88.

*Horn Book* 55 (April 1979): 217; 61 (July 1985): 470; 63 (Jan. 1987): 102.

*Kirkus Reviews* 42 (April 1, 1974): 371.

*Kliatt Young Adult Paperback Book Guide* 25 (Jan. 1991): 57.

*Library Journal* 99 (May 1974): 1450, 1480.

*New Statesman* 89 (May 23, 1975): 694.

*New York Times Book Review* (May 5, 1974): 15; (June 2, 1974): 38; (Nov. 3, 1974): 52; (Dec. 1, 1974): 76.

*Publishers Weekly* 205 (April 15, 1974): 52.

*School Library Journal* 20 (May 1974): 62; 29 (Nov. 1982): 35; 33 (Aug. 1987): 28; 36 (Dec. 1990): 39.

*Top of the News* 31 (April 1975): 331; 40 (Winter 1984): 126.

*Washington Post Book World,* May 19, 1974.

## Articles about This Book

*ALAN Review* 12, no. 2 (Winter 1985): 1–45.

## Background

Campbell, Patricia J. *Presenting Robert Cormier.* Boston: Twayne, 1985.

Caywood, Carolyn. "Time out of Mind: A Few Authors Give Teen Readers the Opportunity to Consider Time as a Construct of the Human Mind." *School Library Journal* 38 (Sept. 1992): 158.

Cormier, Robert. "A Fragile Triumph." *School Library Journal* 37 (Sept. 1991): 184.

Kelly, Patricia. "An Interview with Robert Cormier." *Journal of Youth Services in Libraries* 7 (Fall 1993): 57.

"Looking Backward: Trying to Find the Classic Young Adult Novel." *English Journal* 69 (Sept. 1980): 86–89.

Needham, Nancy R. "Reading Level: Grade 7–Adult." *NEA Today* 7 (May/June 1989): 33.

Probst, Robert E. *Adolescent Literature: Response and Analysis.* Columbus, Ohio: Charles E. Merrill Publishing, 1984. pp. 132–34.

Romano, Tom. "Author's Insights: Turning Teenagers into Readers and Writers." *English Journal* 81 (Nov. 1992): 96.

Schwartz, Sheila. *Teaching Adolescent Literature.* Rochelle Park, N.J.: Hayden Book Company, 1979. pp. 140–42.

Sutton, Roger. "Kind of a Funny Dichotomy: A Conversation with Robert Cormier." *School Library Journal* 37 (June 1991): 28.

## Awards and Prizes

ALAN Award, 1983, to Robert Cormier for the body of his work, presented by the Assembly on Literature for Adolescents, National Council of Teachers of English

Best of the Best Books for Young Adults, 1983

Lewis Carroll Shelf Award, 1979

Margaret A. Edwards Award, presented for the body of Cormier's work by the Young Adult Library Services Association of the American Library Association, 1991

Media and Methods Maxi Award, 1976, for best paperback, presented by *Media and Methods Magazine*

Nothin' But the Best: Best of the Best Books for Young Adults, 1988

Outstanding Books of 1974, presented by the *New York Times*

Still Alive: Best of the Best Books for Young Adults, 1975

## References about the Author

*Authors and Artists for Young Adults.* Vol. 3. Detroit: Gale, 1990.

*Children's Literature Review.* Detroit: Gale, 1987. v. 12, pp. 114–39.

*Contemporary Authors, New Revision Series.* Vol. 23. Detroit: Gale, 1988.

*Contemporary Literary Criticism.* Vol. 30. Detroit: Gale, 1984.

*Magill's Survey of American Literature.* Ed. Frank N. Magill. North Bellmore, N.Y.: Marshall Cavendish, 1991.

*Something about the Author.* Detroit: Gale, 1986. v. 45, pp. 59–65.

## Sources Recommending This Book

Carter, Betty. *Best Books for Young Adults: The History, the Selections, the Romance.* Chicago: American Library Association, 1994. pp. 91, 158, 173, 174, 175.

Gillespie, John T., ed. *Best Books for Junior High Readers.* New Providence, N.J.: R. R. Bowker, 1991. p. 47.

Gillespie, John T., ed. *Best Books for Senior High Readers.* New Providence, N.J.: R. R. Bowker, 1991.

Kaywell, Joan F. *Adolescents at Risk: A Guide to Fiction and Nonfiction for Young Adults, Parents and Professionals.* Westport, Conn.: Greenwood, 1993. pp. 164, 208.

Spencer, Pam. *What Do Young Adults Read Next? A Reader's Guide to Fiction for Young Adults.* Detroit: Gale, 1994. pp. 111, 112, 479.

Young Adult Library Services Association. *Outstanding Books for the College Bound: Choices for a Generation.* Chicago: American Library Association, 1996.

*The Young Adult Reader's Adviser.* Vol. 1, *The Best in Literature and Language Arts, Mathematics, and Computer Science.* Ed. Myra Immell. New Providence, N.J.: R. R. Bowker, 1992. pp. 212–13.

Zvirin, Stephanie. *Best Years of Their Lives: A Resource Guide for Teenagers in Crisis.* 2nd ed. Chicago: American Library Association, 1996. p. 24.

## Audiovisual Resources

*The Chocolate War.* 4-track, 1⅞ cassette. 390 min. Producer and distributor: Recorded Books, Inc., 270 Skipjack Road, Prince Frederick, MD 20678; (800) 638-1304. Same format also distributed by Dercum Audio, Inc., 910 West Chester, PA 19380; (213) 430-8889.

*The Chocolate War.* 1-track, 1⅞ cassette. Series title: Young Adult Recordings Series. Producer: Miller-Brody Productions, Inc., 2700 Coolidge Ave., Los Angeles, CA 90064; (213) 478-3379. Distributor: Random House, Inc., 400 Hahn Road, Westminster, MD 21157; (800) 726-0600.

# Christine

New York: Viking Press, 1983

Skinny, pimply faced Arnie Cunningham buys a decrepit 1958 Plymouth Fury named Christine from Roland LeBay, an unpleasant World War II veteran, who dies unmourned shortly thereafter. Arnie's fascination with the car initially seems no more than a teenage boy's typical love of anything automotive. But Arnie is a kid who has been repeatedly bullied throughout childhood and adolescence by his parents as well as his classmates. Always outnumbered and rendered powerless, Arnie begins to find new strength through a peculiar alliance with Christine. As he restores the car to its original glory—at a mysteriously quick pace—his acne clears up, he begins to date the prettiest girl in school, and he stands up to his tormentors—both at home and in the school yard. When a group of Arnie's enemies trash Christine, each soon dies a gruesome death; and a horrifying cycle of revenge and murder unfolds in a small Pennsylvania town.

Narrated retrospectively by Arnie's best friend, Dennis, King's novel's greatest strength and its greatest appeal for young adult readers is the emotional resonance of the boys' friendship. As the truth of Arnie's obsession with Christine becomes evident to Dennis—that his best friend is pos-

sessed by the not-so-dead LeBay—Dennis does his best to save Arnie, even while he falls in love with Arnie's girl.

King knows teenagers well. He portrays a world of intense emotion, male conflict, competition for status, and the milestones through which boys must pass to become men, including negotiating that critically important first sexual relationship. Invoking the major icons of adolescent culture—popular music, cars, friendship, and sex—and mixing them into a potent brew that includes the supernatural, King tells a story that rings true with young adults.

Challenged for its explicit language and depictions of adolescent sexual relationships, the novel also draws connections between Arnie's overly controlling parents and his eventual homicidal rage. King's descriptions of Christine's victims' deaths, as well as those of Roland LeBay in various states of posthumous decay, are vintage King.

## Challenges

In 1994, challenged, along with eight other Stephen King novels, in Bismarck, North Dakota, by a local minister and a school board member because of "age appropriateness."

Challenged at the Webber Township (Bluford, Ill.) High School Library, along with all other Stephen King novels, in 1993.

Removed from the Livingston (Mont.) Middle School Library (1990) because it was deemed not "suitable for intended audience," owing to violence, explicit sex, and inappropriate language.

In 1989, after a parent complained about offensive passages, the book was removed from the Washington Middle School Library in Meriden, Connecticut.

## Reviews

*Booklist* 79 (Feb. 1, 1983): 697–98.

*English Journal* 73 (Dec. 1984): 66.

*Extrapolation* 29 (Summer 1988): 144.

*Horn Book* 59 (Aug. 1983): 479.

*Kirkus Reviews* 51 (Feb. 1, 1988): 138.

*Kliatt Paperback Book Guide* 18 (Spring 1984): 19.

*Library Journal* 108 (March 1, 1983): 517.

*Los Angeles Times Book Review* (May 8, 1983): 3.

*Magazine of Fantasy and Science Fiction* 65 (Aug. 1983): 15.

*Newsweek* 101 (May 2, 1983): 76.

*New York Times* 132 (April 12, 1983): 27.

*New York Times Book Review* 88 (April 3, 1983): 12.

*Publishers Weekly* 223 (Feb. 25, 1983): 80; 224 (Oct. 7, 1983): 93.

*Science Fiction & Fantasy Book Review* (July 1983): 35.

*Science Fiction Review* 12 (Nov. 1983): 39.

*Voice of Youth Advocates* 6 (Aug. 1983): 146.

*West Coast Review of Books* 9 (May 1983): 36.

## Sources Recommending This Book

*Fiction Catalog,* 13th ed. Eds. Juliette Yaakov and John Greenfieldt. New York: H. W. Wilson, 1996. p. 365.

Gillespie, John T., ed. *Best Books for Senior High Readers.* New Providence, N.J.: R. R. Bowker, 1991. p. 89.

Spencer, Pam. *What Do Young Adults Read Next? A Reader's Guide to Fiction for Young Adults.* Detroit: Gale, 1994. p. 317.

*The Young Adult Reader's Adviser.* Vol. 1, *The Best in Literature and Language Arts, Mathematics, and Computer Science.* Ed. Myra Immell. New Providence, N.J.: R. R. Bowker, 1992. p. 249.

## References about the Author

*Authors and Artists for Young Adults.* Vol. 1. Detroit: Gale, 1989.

*Benet's Reader's Encyclopedia.* 3rd ed. New York: Harper, 1987.

*Contemporary Authors, New Revision Series.* Vol. 30. Detroit: Gale, 1990.

*Contemporary Literary Criticism.* Vol. 61. Detroit: Gale, 1990.

*Cyclopedia of World Authors II.* Ed. Frank N. Magill. Pasadena, Calif.: Salem, 1989.

*Novels and Novelists: A Guide to the World of Fiction.* Ed. Martin Seymour-Smith. New York: St. Martin's, 1980.

*Penguin Encyclopedia of Horror and the Supernatural.* Ed. Jack Sullivan. New York: Viking Penguin, 1986.

*Science Fiction and Fantasy Literature, 1975–1991.* Detroit: Gale, 1992.

*Something about the Author.* Vol. 55. Detroit: Gale, 1989.

## Audiovisual Resources

*Christine.* Motion picture. Columbia Pictures, 1983.

# The Clan of the Cave Bear

New York: Crown, 1980

After a violent earthquake orphans a five-year-old prehistoric girl, she lives alone in a forest (and survives an attack by a lion) until she finds a tribe of humans. The Clan of the Cave Bear takes her in, despite the fact that she looks and acts so differently from them. She is cared for by the Clan's medicine woman, Iza, and her brother, Creb, the Clan magician, who discover the girl's name is Ayla and who teach her the customs and language of the Clan.

While Ayla does her best to conform to the Clan's code, she is different from them, one of the Others, as the Clan calls her kind. She is taller, blond, and blue-eyed; and her brain seems to be constructed differently. Creb divines that Ayla's totem is the lion, the strongest totem of all—save the cave bear—and unheard of for a female. Ayla's powers of speech are more developed than those of the Clan, who communicate largely through gesture. Ayla is also unable to tap into the powerful shared racial memories of the Clan, which gets her into trouble when she becomes adept at hunting, a skill not only forbidden women, but one that would not occur to them to pursue.

Ayla's prowess with a slingshot incurs the jealousy of Broud, the proud and hot-tempered son of the Clan leader. After years of simmering envy and punishing Ayla in any way he could, Broud repeatedly assaults Ayla in a way that contemporary readers will recognize as rape but is acceptable as Clan tradition; any female must submit to any male whenever he makes a special gesture. When Ayla becomes pregnant as a result of the rape, it is regarded as a miracle by the Clan, who assumed that her differentness rendered her incapable of bearing children and who have not made the connection between sexual intercourse and reproduction. After an earthquake destroys the Clan's cave, Broud, now leader, blames Ayla, curses her, and expels her from the Clan, forcing her to leave her son behind. Ayla's story is continued in three sequels: *The Valley of Horses, The Mammoth Hunters*, and *The Plains of Passage*.

## Challenges

Challenged at the Berrien Springs, Michigan, High School for use in classrooms and libraries in 1988 because the novel is "vulgar, profane, and sexually explicit."

Banned from the Cascade Middle School library in Eugene, Oregon, in

1992 after a parent complained about a rape scene.

Challenged, but retained on the Moorpark High School recommended reading list in Simi Valley, California, in 1993 despite objections that it contains "hard-core graphic sexual content."

## Reviews

*Booklist* 76 (July 15, 1980): 1638.

*Book World* 10 (Sept. 28, 1980): 6.

*Christian Science Monitor* 76 (Dec. 2, 1983): B3.

*Kirkus Reviews* 48 (July 1, 1980): 846.

*Kliatt Paperback Book Guide* 15 (Fall 1981): 4.

*Library Journal* 105 (Sept. 1, 1980): 1750.

*Locus* 25 (Dec. 1990): 51; 28 (Jan. 1992): 54.

*Ms.* 10 (Dec. 1981): 22; 14 (March 1986): 64.

*New York Times Book Review* 85 (Aug. 31, 1980): 7; 86 (July 26, 1981): 23.

*Publishers Weekly* 218 (July 18, 1980): 47; 219 (June 19, 1981): 98.

*School Library Journal* 27 (Nov. 1980): 91.

*Science Fiction Review* 11 (Nov. 1982): 28.

*Scientific American* 256 (June 1987): 132.

*Voice of Youth Advocates* 14 (Dec. 1991): 297.

*Wilson Library Bulletin* 55 (Nov. 1980): 215.

## Awards and Prizes

Best of the Best Books for Young Adults, 1983

## References About the Author

*Science Fiction Source Book.* Ed. David Wingrove. New York: Van Nostrand Reinhold, 1984.

## Sources Recommending This Book

Carter, Betty. *Best Books for Young Adults: The History, the Selections, the Romance.* Chicago: American Library Association, 1994. p. 80.

*Fiction Catalog,* 13th ed. Eds. Juliette Yaakov and John Greenfieldt. New York: H. W. Wilson, 1996. p. 32.

Gillespie, John T., ed. *Best Books for Senior High Readers.* New Providence, N.J.: R. R. Bowker, 1991. p. 68.

*Growing Up Is Hard to Do.* Ed. Sally Estes. Chicago: Booklist/American Library Association, 1994. p. 5.

Spencer, Pam. *What Do Young Adults Read Next? A Reader's Guide to Fiction for Young Adults.* Detroit: Gale, 1994. pp. 21, 55, 133, 168, 211, 250, 429, 494, 571.

*The Young Adult Reader's Adviser:* Vol. 2, *The Best in Social Sciences, History, Science, and Health.* Ed. Myra Immell. New Providence, N.J.: R. R. Bowker, 1992. p. 277.

## Audiovisual Resources

*The Clan of the Cave Bear.* 4-track, 1⅞ cassette. 720 min. Producer and distributor: Books On Tape, P.O. Box 7900, Newport Beach, CA 92658; (800) 626-3333.

*The Clan of the Cave Bear.* 1-track, 1⅞ cassette. Producer and distributor: Books On Tape, P.O. Box 7900, Newport Beach, CA 92658; (800) 626-3333.

# The Color Purple

New York: Harcourt, Brace, Jovanovich, 1982

One passage in *The Color Purple* seems to illuminate the intent or purpose of Walker's story of two sisters, Celie and Nettie, bound to each other by love and fear, joy and sorrow, and reunited after a separation of 30 years.

> He laugh—Who you think you is?
> he say. You can't curse nobody.
> Look at you. You black, you pore,
> you ugly, you a woman. Goddam,
> he say, you nothing at all.
> (*The Color Purple*, p. 176)

The passage is reflective of what people fear and despise in this book. For people who believe, implicitly, that to be black/poor/ugly/woman is to be nothing—and to be all of these together is to be less than nothing, the lowest thing in Creation—Walker's book is political, social, and sexual heresy. Walker is blaspheming against the accepted order of things. She is daring to say that one can be black/poor/ugly/woman and nonetheless *somebody,* a person of intrinsic dignity and worth. There is no such thing as "trash" if you believe and practice the belief that God is not He or She but It, and that It is everywhere and in everything.

> I'm pore, I'm black, I may be ugly
> and can't cook, a voice says to everything listening. But I'm here.
> (*The Color Purple*, p. 176).

There is nothing new or shocking in the elements of Walker's narrative. It is the angle of approach that is so unsettling. The reader has heard about oppression from the point of view of the oppressors, about racial relations from the dominant race, about religion from those who preach God the Old Man, about marriage from husbands, and about sex from men. But in *The Color Purple* one views these familiar conflicts from the other perspective, from the inside out and the bottom up, and what the reader is forced to see is painful indeed.

Yet out of violence, poverty, oppression, and abuse, Celie, the narrator, creates a life for herself and reaches out with love to those around her. Out of all she has experienced, she emerges strong and enduring. Quilting is the metaphor for this process of growth in the book: Celie takes the ragged scraps of her life and pieces them together with exquisite stitches into a pattern of beauty. For Walker, Celie's life, like her quilts, is beautiful and precious because of the time and effort, the thought and care, that have gone into its making.

## Challenges

Challenged as inappropriate reading for an Oakland, California, high school honors class (1984) due to the work's "sexual and social explicitness" and its "troubling ideas about race relations, man's relationship to God, African history, and human sexuality." After nine months of haggling and delays, a divided Oakland Board of Education gave formal approval for the book's use.

Rejected for purchase by the Hayward, California, school trustees (1985) because of "rough language" and "explicit sex scenes."

Removed from the open shelves of the Newport News, Virginia, school library (1986) because of its "profanity and sexual references" and because the school principal felt it "might incite rape." The book was restricted to a special section accessible only to students over the age of 18 or those who have written permission from a parent.

Because it was "too sexually graphic for a 12-year-old," it was challenged at the public libraries in Saginaw, Michigan, in 1989.

Challenged as a summer youth program reading assignment in Chattanooga, Tennessee (1989), because of its language and "explicitness."

Challenged in Ten Sleep, Wyoming (1990), schools when a request to reconsider the use of the book was presented to the school board. The superintendent said the book was not required reading and the students could choose to change the books they were reading.

Because the main character is raped by her stepfather, the book was challenged as a reading assignment at the New Bern (N.C.) High School in 1992.

Challenged in New Bern, North Carolina (1992). The parents of a tenth-grader who was assigned the book objected to the assignment of the book without providing a choice.

Challenged in Souderton, Pennsylvania (1993), because of explicit language and graphic depiction of sexual encounters and rape. The school board voted to ban the use of the novel in a tenth-grade honors English class. The board rejected the unanimous recommendation to retain the book by the district's curriculum council.

## Reviews

*African American Review* 26 (Spring 1992): 89; 28 (Fall 1994): 411.

*Black American Literature Forum* 22 (Spring 1988): 81.

*Black Enterprise* 12 (Dec. 1982): 30.

*Booklist* 78 (April 15, 1982): 1042; 89 (June 1, 1993): 1865; 94 (Oct. 15, 1994): 416.

*Boston Review* 7 (Oct. 1982): 29.

*Christian Century* 105 (Nov. 16, 1988): 1035.

*Christian Science Monitor* 76 (Feb. 3, 1984): B1.

*Commonweal* 110 (Feb. 11, 1983): 93–94.

*English Journal* 74 (Jan. 1985): 48; 79 (Oct. 1990): 83.

*Essence* 13 (Oct. 1982): 20; 19 (July 1988): 28.

*Journal of Black Studies* 18 (March 1988): 379; 20 (Dec. 1989): 192.

*Kirkus Reviews* 50 (April 15, 1982): 518.

*Library Journal* 107 (June 1, 1982): 1115; 117 (July 1992): 132.

*Modern Fiction Studies* 34 (Spring 1988): 69.

*Nation* 235 (Sept. 4, 1982): 181–84; 235 (Dec. 25, 1982): 696.

*New York Review of Books* 29 (Aug. 12, 1982): 35–36; 34 (Jan. 29, 1987): 17.

*New York Times Book Review* 88 (July 26, 1981): 23.

*New Yorker* 58 (Sept. 6, 1982): 106.

*Newsweek* 99 (June 21, 1982): 67–68.

*Publishers Weekly* 221 (May 14, 1982): 285; 223 (April 29, 1983): 50.

*San Francisco Review of Books* 7 (Summer 1982): 5; 7 (Jan. 1983): 23.

*West Coast Review of Books* 8 (Sept. 1982): 22.

## Articles about This Book

Bradley, D. "Telling the Black Woman's Story." *New York Times Magazine* 133 (Jan. 8, 1984): 24–37.

Harris, Trudier. "On *The Color Purple*, Stereotypes, and Silence." *Black American Literature Forum* 189 (Winter 1984): 155–61.

Pinckney, D. "Black Victims, Black Villains." *New York Review of Books* 34 (Jan. 29, 1987): 17–20.

Stade, George. "Womanist Fiction and Male Characters." *Partisan Review* 52 (1985): 70.

Steinem, Gloria. "Do You Know This Woman? She Knows You: A Profile of Alice Walker." *Ms.* 10 (June 1982): 35–37, 89–94.

Walker, Alice. "Finding Celie's Voice." *Ms.* 14 (Dec. 1985): 71–72 + .

Washington, Mary Helen. "Alice Walker: Her Mother's Gifts." *Ms.* 10 (June 1982): 38.

## Background

Cook, Michael G. "Alice Walker." In *Afro-American Literature in the Twentieth Century; the Achievement of Intimacy.* New Haven, Conn.: Yale University Press, 1984. pp. 133–76.

Davis, T. M. "Alice Walker's Celebration of Self in Southern Generations." In *Women Writers of the Contemporary South.* Edited by Peggy Whitman Prenshaw. Jackson, Miss.: University Press of Mississippi, 1984. pp. 39–53.

Dixon, Melvin. "Keep Me from Sinking Down: Zora Neale Hurston, Alice Walker and Gayl Jones." In *Ride out of the Wilderness; Geography and Identity in Afro-*

*American Literature*. Champaign, Ill.: University of Illinois Press, 1987. pp. 83–120.

Fifer, E. "Alice Walker: The Dialect and Letters of *The Color Purple*." In *Contemporary American Women Writers; Narrative Strategies*. Eds. Catherine Rainwater and William J. Scheick. Lexington, Ky.: University Press of Kentucky, 1985. pp. 155–71.

Light, A. "Fear of the Happy Ending: *The Color Purple*, Reading and Racism." In *Essays and Studies, Volume Forty: Broadening the Context*. Ed. Michael Green, in association with Richard Haggart, for the English Association. Atlantic Highlands, N.J.: Humanities Press, 1987. pp. 103–17.

Parker-Smith, Bettye J. "Alice Walker's Women: In Search of Some Peace of Mind." In *Black Women Writers, 1950–1980: A Critical Evaluation*. Ed. Marl Evans. Garden City, N.Y.: Doubleday, 1984. pp. 478–93.

Pratt, L. H. and Darwell Pratt. *Alice Walker: A Bibliography*. Westport, Conn.: Meckler, 1987.

Tate, Claudia. "Alice Walker." In *Black Women Writers at Work*. Ed. Claudia Tate. New York: Continuum Press, 1983. pp. 175–87.

Walker, Alice. "Writing *The Color Purple*." In *In Search of Our Mother's Gardens; Womanist Prose*. New York: Harcourt, 1983. pp. 355–60.

Wesley, Richard. "*The Color Purple* Debate: Reading between the Lines." *Ms.* 15 (Sept. 1986): 62, 90–92.

## Awards and Prizes

American Book Award for Fiction, 1983

National Book Award, 1983

Pulitzer Prize for Fiction, 1983

## References about the Author

*American Women Writers: A Critical Reference Guide, from Colonial Times to the Present*. 4 vols. Ed. Lina Mainiers. New York: Frederick Ungar, 1982. pp. 313–15.

*Contemporary Authors, First Revision Series*. Detroit: Gale, 1979. v. 37–40, pp. 582–83.

*Contemporary Authors, New Revision Series*. Detroit: Gale, 1983. v. 9, pp. 514–17.

*Contemporary Literary Criticism*. Detroit: Gale, 1976. v. 5, pp. 476–77; v. 6, pp. 553–54; v. 9, pp. 557–58; v. 27, pp. 448–54; v. 46, pp. 422–32.

*Something about the Author*. Detroit: Gale, 1983. v. 31, pp. 177–79.

## Sources Recommending This Book

*Fiction Catalog*, 13th ed. Eds. Juliette Yaakov and John Greenfieldt. New York: H. W. Wilson, 1996. p. 677.

Gillespie, John T., ed. *Best Books for Senior High Readers.* New Providence, N.J.: R. R. Bowker, 1991. p. 38.

*Growing Up Is Hard to Do.* Ed. Sally Estes. Chicago: Booklist/American Library Association, 1994, p. 53.

*The Reader's Advisor: The Best in Reference Works, British Literature & American Literature.* 14th ed. 3 vols. New York: R. R. Bowker, 1994. v. 1, p. 1064.

Rochman, Hazel. *Against Borders: Promoting Books for a Multicultural World.* Chicago: Booklist/American Library Association, 1993, p. 176.

*Senior High School Library Catalog.* 14th ed. New York: H. W. Wilson, 1992. p. 727.

*Top One Hundred Countdown: Best of the Best Books for Young Adults, 1969–1994.* Chicago: American Library Association, 1995.

Young Adult Library Services Association. *Outstanding Books for the College Bound: Choices for a Generation.* Chicago: American Library Association, 1996.

*The Young Adult Reader's Adviser.* Vol. 1, *The Best in Literature and Language Arts, Mathematics, and Computer Science.* Ed. Myra Immell. New Providence, N.J.: R. R. Bowker, 1992. v. 1, pp. 296–97.

## Audiovisual Resources

*The Color Purple.* Warner Bros. 1985.

*The Color Purple.* 1/2-inch videocassette (VHS). 154 min. Producer and distributor: Guidance Associates, 90 S. Bedford Rd., Mt. Kisco, NY 10549; (800) 431-1242; (914) 666-4100, fax: (914) 666-5319.

# A Day No Pigs Would Die

New York: Knopf, 1973

Through his relationship with his hard-working father, 12-year-old Rob learns to cope with the harshness of Shaker life and emerges a more mature person. This book is a plainspoken work about people poor in worldly possessions but rich in understanding of and appreciation for the basic and necessary acts of life. Robert Newton Peck's book, *A Day No Pigs Would Die*, belongs to that almost-defunct school of American literature called regionalism. Peck has provided his readers with a window onto a landscape that has largely disappeared from the contemporary literary scene—those isolated and impoverished but proud pockets of rural America that constituted the heart and soul of our literary self-consciousness until 40 years ago.

*A Day No Pigs Would Die*, through the intensity of its first-person narration and the pungency of its colloquial language, immerses readers in the earthy and unsparing struggle of working a living out of the land. It is a conservative book, honoring the virtues and values of a sterner, stricter creed. Yet it also shows that strong convictions and intolerance of others need not go hand-in-hand. It shows how people of good will can agree to differ and still live in harmony. It argues that compassion and forgiveness

are just as important as justice. And it demonstrates how growth and maturity can result not only from some great and wrenching change, but from the accumulation of small but significant choices made in the ordinary course of everyday life.

Those passages that frankly describe men and beasts behaving according to their natural instincts are essential to Peck's avowed intention of providing his readers with an honest and unvarnished account of life lived close to nature. In this regard, *A Day No Pigs Would Die* is an excellent example of literary realism and provides an opportunity to examine a real life experience, which formed what are called traditional American values.

This book is a tribute, honest, unsparing, and loving, written by a son to the father he honors but never idolizes.

## Challenges

Challenged in the Jefferson County (Colo.) school libraries (1988) because "it is bigoted against Baptists and women and depicts violence, hatred, animal cruelty, and murder."

Because it contains language and subject matter that set bad examples and give students negative views of life, the book was challenged in the Hawinton and Burlington (Conn.) schools in 1990.

Challenged at the Sherwood Elementary School in Melbourne, Florida (1993), because the book could give the "impression that rape and violence are acceptable." The comment was made in reference to a descriptive passage about a boar mating a sow in the barnyard.

After a parent "objected to graphic passages dealing with sexuality in the book," the book was challenged, but retained, on the shelves of Waupaca (Wis.) school libraries in 1994.

Removed from seventh-grade classes at Payson (Utah) Middle School in 1994 after several parents "had problems with language, with animal breeding, and with a scene that involves an infant grave exhumation."

## Reviews

*Atlantic Monthly* 231 (April 1973): 114.

*Booklist* 82 (March 1, 1986): 975; 87 (Feb. 15, 1991): 1185; 88 (Feb. 15, 1992): 1101; 90 (June 1, 1994): 1799.

*Bulletin of the Center for Children's Books* 26 (May 1973): 142.

*Christian Science Monitor* 65 (Jan. 17, 1973): 11.

*Emergency Librarian* 9 (Jan. 1982): 17.

*English Journal* 69 (Sept. 1980): 87.

*Horn Book* 49 (Oct. 1973): 472.

*Kirkus Reviews* 40 (Oct. 15, 1972): 1215; 40 (Nov. 1, 1972): 1258.

*Library Journal* 97 (Nov. 15, 1972): 3728; 98 (March 15, 1973): 1022.

*New York Times* 122 (Jan. 4, 1973): 35.

*New York Times Book Review* (May 13, 1973): 37.

*New Yorker* 48 (Feb. 3, 1973): 100.

*Newsweek* 81 (March 12, 1973): 96.

*Publishers Weekly* 202 (Oct. 30, 1972): 49; 204 (Oct. 22, 1973): 112.

*Saturday Review* 1 (Jan. 13, 1973): 66.

*School Library Journal* 29 (Aug. 1983): 27.

*Times Literary Supplement*, Aug. 17, 1973, p. 945.

*Wilson Library Bulletin* 49 (March 1975): 517.

## Awards and Prizes

Colorado Children's Book Award, presented by the Colorado Library Association, 1977

Margaret A. Edwards Award, presented for the body of Peck's work by the Young Adult Library Services Association of the American Library Association, 1990

Media and Methods Maxi Award for best paperback presented by *Media and Methods Magazine*, 1975

Still Alive: Best of the Best Books for Young Adults, 1975

## References about the Author

*Contemporary Authors.* Detroit: Gale, 1979. v. 81–84, pp. 442–43.

*Something about the Author.* Detroit: Gale, 1980. v. 21, pp. 113–14.

## Sources Recommending This Book

Carter, Betty. *Best Books for Young Adults: The History, the Selections, the Romance.* Chicago: American Library Association, 1994. pp. 133, 158, 174.

*Fiction Catalog.* 13th ed. Eds. Juliette Yaakov and John Greenfieldt. New York: H. W. Wilson, 1996. p. 507.

*Fiction for Youth: A Guide to Recommended Books.* 2nd ed. Ed. Lillian L. Shapiro. New York: Neal-Schuman Publishers, 1986. p. 151.

Gillespie, John T., ed. *Best Books for Junior High Readers.* New Providence, N.J.: R. R. Bowker, 1991. p. 31.

*Growing Up Is Hard to Do.* Ed. Sally Estes. Chicago: Booklist/American Library Association, 1994. pp. 14, 39, 57.

Helbig, Alethea K., and Agnes Regan Perkins. *Dictionary of American Children's Fiction, 1960–1984: Recent Books of Recognized Merit.* New York: Greenwood, 1986. pp. 149–50.

*Junior High School Library Catalog.* 6th ed. Ed. Juliette Yaakov. New York: H. W. Wilson, 1990. p. 402.

Kaywell, Joan F. *Adolescents at Risk: A Guide to Fiction and Nonfiction for Young Adults, Parents and Professionals.* Westport, Conn.: Greenwood, 1993. p. 225.

*Senior High School Library Catalog.* 14th ed. Eds. Brenda Smith and Juliette Yaakov. New York: H. W. Wilson, 1992. p. 713.

Spencer, Pam. *What Do Young Adults Read Next? A Reader's Guide to Fiction for Young Adults.* Detroit: Gale, 1994. pp. 406, 439.

## Audiovisual Resources

*A Day No Pigs Would Die.* 4-track, 1⅞ cassette. Distributor: Dercum Audio, Inc., 910 Waltz Road, West Chester, PA 19380; (215) 430-8889. Also distributed by A. W. Peller and Assoc., Inc., Educational Materials, 210 Sixth Ave., P.O. Box 106, Hawthorne, NJ 07507; (800) 451-7450.

*A Day No Pigs Would Die.* Also on 4-track, 1⅞ cassette, from A. W. Peller. Series title: Large-Print Middle Grade Read-Alongs Series. This offers large print for reluctant readers, ESL students, and the visually impaired, as well as appropriately paced read-along cassettes.

*A Day No Pigs Would Die.* 16mm film, 3/4- or 1/2-inch video. Series title: "Books Our Children Read." Producer and distributor: Films Incorporated Video, 5547 N. Ravenswood Ave., Chicago, IL 60640-1199; (800) 323-4222.

## WALTER DEAN MYERS

# Fallen Angels

New York: Scholastic, 1988

Richie Perry, a 17-year-old resident of Harlem, decides the army might be an improvement over the mean streets of his neighborhood. He enlists, hoping his medical profile will catch up with him before he ends up "in country" and that his bad knee will keep him from seeing action. Richie survives his stint in Vietnam in 1967, shortly before the Tet Offensive and the war's escalation—but not until he has earned his second Purple Heart, seen his buddies and his sergeant die, and killed enemy soldiers no older than himself.

Most of the young men in Richie's company are teenagers, and Richie develops a friendship with another African American, a soldier from Chicago nicknamed Peewee. Myers tells of the racial prejudice encountered by black soldiers and of the loyalty that develops among the men regardless of race or rumored sexual orientation. Myers's prose is peppered with racial epithets, including those derogatory terms used to indicate the Vietnamese, as well as with obscenities.

Other issues in the novel that subject it to censorship include its violence and its graphic descriptions of war's atrocities and the absurdity and waste of war in general, but particularly of the Vietnam War. A theme that runs through the novel is the contrast between foxhole religious conversion and true spiritual growth, which is accompanied by the ability to rise above the death and destruction of war.

Another theme about which Myers writes so eloquently is the dissociation Richie experiences in the face of the horrors he confronts in battle and the implied long-term effects it will have on him. He wonders if he will survive to love a woman, to grow up, to become a man.

## Challenges

Because of its use of profane language, the book was challenged in the Bluffton (Ohio) schools in 1990.

Restricted as supplemental classroom reading material at the Jackson County (Ga.) High School in 1992 because of undesirable language and sensitive material.

Challenged at the West Chester (Pa.) schools (1994).

## Reviews

*Book Report* 7 (Sept. 1988): 36; 7 (Nov. 1988): 24; 8 (Sept. 1989): 67; 12 (Jan. 1994): 24.

*Booklist* 84 (April 15, 1988): 1419; 86 (Feb. 1, 1990): 1098; 86 (May 1, 1990): 1697; 87 (Jan. 15, 1991): 1021; 90 (Oct. 1, 1993): 244.

*Books for Keeps* 38 (Jan. 1992): 10.

*Bulletin of the Center for Children's Books* 41 (April 1988): 163.

*Children's Book Review Service* 16 (June 1988): 125.

*Emergency Librarian* 16 (Nov. 1988): 48; 17 (Nov. 1989): 63.

*English Journal* 77 (Dec. 1988): 70; 79 (March 1990): 79; 82 (Sept. 1993): 43.

*Horn Book* 64 (July 1988): 503.

*Journal of Reading* 32 (April 1989): 665; 33 (Dec. 1989): 231; 34 (Nov. 1990): 205.

*Junior Bookshelf* 54 (Aug. 1990): 198.

*Kirkus Reviews* 56 (May 1, 1988): 696.

*New York Times Book Review* 94 (Jan. 22, 1989): 29.

*Publishers Weekly* 233 (May 13, 1988): 277; 235 (Jan. 6, 1989): 52; 235 (June 9, 1989): 72.

*School Librarian* 38 (Aug. 1990): 118.

*School Library Journal* 34 (June 1988): 118; 35 (Oct. 1988): 41; 35 (Nov. 1988): 53; 35 (Feb. 1989): 31; 36 (Dec. 1990): 40; 37 (April 1991): 44.

*Tribune Books* Chicago (Nov. 13, 1988): 6.

*Voice of Youth Advocates* 11 (Aug. 1988): 133; 12 (Feb. 1990): 334; 17 (June 1994): 68.

*Wilson Library Bulletin* 62 (March 1988): 76; 64 (Sept. 1989): 5.

## Awards and Prizes

Coretta Scott King Award, Best Book, 1989

Margaret A. Edwards Award, presented for the body of Walter Dean Myers' work by the Young Adult Library Services Association of the American Library Association, 1994

## Sources Recommending This Book

Carter, Betty. *Best Books for Young Adults: The History, the Selections, the Romance.* Chicago: American Library Association, 1994. pp. 128, 168.

*The Best in Children's Books, 1985–90.* Eds. Zena Sutherland, Betsy Hearne, and Roger Sutton. Chicago: University of Chicago Press, 1991. p. 300.

Gillespie, John T., ed. *Best Books for Senior High Readers.* New Providence, N.J.: R. R. Bowker, 1991. p. 86.

Rochman, Hazel. *Against Borders: Promoting Books for a Multicultural World.* Chicago: Booklist/ American Library Association, 1993. pp. 80, 81, 169, 174.

Spencer, Pam. *What Do Young Adults Read Next? A Reader's Guide to Fiction for Young Adults.* Detroit: Gale, 1994. pp. 11, 27, 151, 364, 374–75, 376, 386, 389, 452.

Zvirin, Stephanie. *Best Years of Their Lives: A Resource Guide for*

*Teenagers in Crisis*. 2nd ed. Chicago: American Library Association, 1996. p. 39.

## References about the Author

*Authors and Artists for Young Adults*. Vol. 4. Detroit: Gale, 1990.

*Contemporary Authors, New Revision Series*. Vol. 20. Detroit: Gale, 1987.

Rollock, Barbara. *Black Authors and Illustrators of Children's Books*. Garland Reference Library of the Humanities. Vol. 660. New York: Garland, 1988.

Ward, Martha E., and others. *Authors of Books for Young People*. 3rd ed. Metuchen, N.J.: Scarecrow, 1990.

## V. C. ANDREWS

# Flowers in the Attic

New York: Simon and Schuster, 1979

When their father is killed in a car accident, the four Dollanganger children are hidden for several years by their mother in their grandparents' attic. The older children, Chris and Cathy, initially believe their mother when she tells them she is attending secretarial school and will soon receive her inheritance from her dying father. They care for and try to educate their younger siblings, the five-year-old twins, Cory and Carrie. Gradually, however, they learn that their mother was their father's niece and that she had been disinherited when she eloped with him. Even worse, they eventually discover that she has abandoned them for a huge fortune and, worst of all, that she has been poisoning them with arsenic. Cory dies as the result of the arsenic. The three surviving children escape from the attic, but not before Chris rapes Cathy in a fit of passion. Narrated by Cathy, the novel recounts her feelings about maturing, her changing body, and her ultimate loss of faith in God because of her imprisonment.

This novel stretches the reader's credibility to the utmost, is awkwardly written, and drags interminably to an anticlimactic ending. But in spite of stilted prose and little action, this novel is widely read by young adults.

Horror is a part of its appeal, but its main draw is sex. And not the healthy sex-is-really-okay stance taken by Judy Blume in *Forever*, but incestuous, forbidden sex, with purple descriptions of unrequited lust.

With the children trapped in an attic, unloved by their parents, and forced to make the best of a bad situation, Andrews' novel is a fairy tale of the adolescent's dilemma—forced to be dependent on family while longing for independence and sexual release.

## Challenges

Because the book contains offensive passages concerning incest and sexual intercourse, it was challenged at the Richmond (R.I.) High School in 1983.

Removed from Oconee County (Ga.) school libraries in (1994) "due to the filthiness of the material." At a later date, the school board voted unanimously to rescind its order to remove the book but then rescinded that action and ordered the book removed.

## Reviews

*Book World* 9 (Nov. 4, 1979): 14.
*Publishers Weekly* 216 (Oct. 1, 1979): 85.

*School Library Journal* 30 (Sept. 1983): 54.

*Voice of Youth Advocates* 6 (Dec. 1983): 265.

## References about the Author

*Something about the Author.* Detroit: Gale, 1988. v. 50, p. 29.

## Sources Recommending This Book

Gillespie, John T., ed. *Best Books for Senior High Readers.* New Providence, N.J.: R. R. Bowker, 1991. p. 86.

*The Reader's Advisor: The Best in Reference Works, British Literature & American Literature.* 14th ed. Ed. Marion Sader. 3 vols. New York: R. R. Bowker, 1994. v. 1, pp. 1239–40.

## Audiovisual Resources

*Garden of the Shadows.* 4-track, $1\frac{7}{8}$ cassette. 720 min. Series title: Dollanganger Series. Books On Tape, P.O. Box 7900, Newport Beach, CA 92658; (800) 626-3333.

## JUDY BLUME

# Forever

New York: Bradbury Press, 1975

Katherine, the heroine of *Forever*, experiences turmoil, changes, romance, and loss during the course of her senior year in high school. By the end of the year (and the story's conclusion), she has experienced and accepted both the pains and the pleasures of growth and has found a new level of maturity.

She has outgrown her relationship with her steady boyfriend, Michael, but the relationship is one she will remember and treasure.

The story contains specific descriptions of sexual acts and the language is explicit. Blume describes, with honesty leavened by humor, what "first love" feels like at the moment it is experienced. She emphasizes also the responsibilities of both partners in a love affair by incorporating frank discussions of sexually transmitted diseases (excluding AIDS), masturbation, condoms, and birth-control methods. Katherine and Michael behave sensibly and take precautions to protect themselves.

Their relationship is not carried out in a state of blissful unawareness. They are also asked to deal with peer pressure, suicide, and the death of a loved one.

The affair ends gently, as Katherine and Michael move on in different directions. No one gets hurt, and no one gets left behind. Blume takes pains to show that love and happiness in human relationships are processes of continuing growth and change that have nothing to do with the fairy-tale fantasy of "happily forever after."

## Challenges

Challenged at the Midvalley Junior-Senior High School in Scranton, Pennsylvania, in 1982, because it contained "four-letter words and talked about masturbation, birth control, and disobedience to parents."

Challenged at the Park Hill, Missouri, South Junior High School Library in 1982, where it was housed on restricted shelves because the book promotes "the stranglehold of humanism on life in America."

Challenged at the Orlando, Florida, schools in 1982.

Challenged at the Akron, Ohio, School District libraries in 1983.

Challenged at the Howard-Suamico, (Wis.) High School in 1983 because "it demoralizes marital sex."

Challenged and eventually moved from the Holdredge, Nebraska, Public Library young adult section to the adult section in 1984 because the

**43**

"book is pornographic and does not promote the sanctity of family life."

Challenged at the Cedar Rapids, Iowa, Public Library in 1984 because it is "pornography and explores areas God didn't intend to explore outside of marriage."

Placed on a restricted shelf by the Patrick County, Virginia, School Board in 1986.

Challenged at the Campbell County, Wyoming, school libraries in 1986 because it is "pornographic" and would encourage young readers "to experiment with sexual encounters."

Challenged at the Moreno Valley, California, Unified School District libraries in 1987 because it "contains profanity, sexual situations, and themes that allegedly encourage disrespectful behavior."

Challenged at the Marshwood Junior High School classroom library in Eliot, Maine, in 1987 because the "book does not paint a responsible role of parents"; its "cast of sex-minded teenagers is not typical of high schoolers today"; and the "pornographic sexual exploits (in the book) are unsuitable for junior high school role models."

The West Hernando, Florida, Middle School principal in 1988 recommended that Blume's novel be removed from school shelves because it is "inappropriate."

Placed on reserve at the Herrin, Illinois, Junior High School library in 1992 and can be checked out only with a parent's written permission because the novel is "sexually provocative reading."

Removed from the Frost Junior High School Library in Schaumburg, Illinois, in 1993 because "it's basically a sexual 'how-to-do' book for junior high students. It glamorizes [sex] and puts ideas in their heads."

Placed on the "parental permission shelf" at the Rib Lake, Wisconsin, high school libraries in 1993 after Superintendent Ray Parks filed a "request for reconsideration" because he found the book "sexually explicit." It was subsequently confiscated by the high school principal in 1993. A federal jury in Madison, Wisconsin, awarded $394,560 to a former Rib Lake High School guidance counselor after finding that his contract was not renewed in retaliation for speaking out against the district's book policy. The counselor had criticized the decision of the Rib Lake High School principal to restrict student access to the novel.

Removed from Mediapolis, Iowa, School District libraries in 1994 because it "does not promote abstinence and monogamous relationships [and] lacks any aesthetic, literary, or social value." Returned to shelves a month later but accessible only to high schoolers.

## Reviews

*Booklist* 72 (Oct. 15, 1975): 291.

*Bulletin of the Center for Children's Books* 29 (March 1976): 106.

*Children's Literature in Education* 20 (June 1989): 81.

*English Journal* 65 (March 1976): 90; 66 (Jan. 1977): 64; 67 (May 1978): 90.

*Horn Book* 61 (Jan. 1985): 86.

*Kirkus Reviews* 43 (Oct. 1, 1975): 1136.

*Mother Jones* 5 (Jan. 1980): 60.

*Ms.* 16 (Aug. 1987): 160.

*New Statesman* 92 (Nov. 5, 1976): 644.

*New York Times Book Review* (Dec. 28, 1975): 20.

*Publishers Weekly* 208 (Aug. 18, 1975): 63.

*School Librarian* 32 (Sept. 1984): 209.

*School Library Journal* 22 (Nov. 1975): 95.

*Times Literary Supplement* (Oct. l, 1976): 1238.

*Top of the News* 37 (Fall 1980): 57.

## Articles about this Book

Forman, Jack. "Young Adult Books: 'Watch out for #1'." *Horn Book* 61 (Jan.–Feb. 1985): 85.

McNulty, Faith. "Children's Books for Christmas." *New Yorker* 59 (Dec. 5, 1983): 191.

Maynard, Joyce. "Coming of Age with Judy Blume." *New York Times Magazine* (Dec. 3, 1978): 80 + .

Thompson, Susan. "Images of Adolescence: Part I." *Signal* 34 (1981): 5759.

## Background

Lee, Betsy. *Judy Blume's Story*. Minneapolis, Minn.: Dillon, 1981.

## Awards and Prizes

Margaret A. Edwards Award, presented to Blume for *Forever* by the Young Adult Library Services Association of the American Library Association, 1996

## References about the Author

*Contemporary Authors*. Detroit: Gale, 1978. v. 29–32R, p. 72.

*Contemporary Authors, New Revision Series*. Detroit: Gale, 1984. v. 13, pp. 59–62.

*Contemporary Literary Criticism*. Detroit: Gale, 1980. v. 12, pp. 44–48; v. 30, pp. 20–25.

*Current Biography Yearbook, 1980*. Ed. Charles Moritz. New York: Wilson, 1981. pp. 17–20.

*Fourth Book of Junior Authors and Illustrators*. Ed. Doris De Montreville. New York: H. W. Wilson, 1978. pp. 46–47.

*Something about the Author*. Detroit: Gale. v. 2, pp. 31–32; v. 31, pp. 28–34.

## Sources Recommending This Book

*Books for You: A Booklist for Senior High Students*. Ed. Donald R. Gallo. Committee on the Senior High School Booklist. Urbana, Ill.: National Council of Teachers of English, 1985. p. 268.

Gillespie, John T., ed. *Best Books for Senior High Readers.* New Providence, N.J.: R. R. Bowker, 1991. p. 39.

*High-Low Handbook: Encouraging Literacy in the 1990s.* 3rd ed. Comp. and ed. Ellen V. LiBretto. New York: Bowker, 1990. p. 236.

Kaywell, Joan F. *Adolescents at Risk: A Guide to Fiction and Nonfiction for Young Adults, Parents and Professionals.* Westport, Conn.: Greenwood, 1993. p. 184.

Spencer, Pam. *What Do Young Adults Read Next? A Reader's Guide to Fiction for Young Adults.* Detroit: Gale, 1994. p. 80.

*Top One Hundred Countdown: Best of the Best Books for Young Adults, 1969–1994.* Chicago: American Library Association, 1995.

*The Young Adult Reader's Adviser.* Vol. 1, *The Best in Literature and Language Arts, Mathematics, and Computer Science.* Ed. Myra Immell. New Providence, N.J.: R. R. Bowker, 1992. p. 201.

## Audiovisual Resources

*Forever.* CBS-TV, 1978.

ANONYMOUS

# Go Ask Alice

Englewood Cliffs, N.J.: Prentice-Hall, 1971

Alleged to have been based on an actual diary of a teenage girl who became a drug addict and died of an overdose, *Go Ask Alice* has been a controversial title throughout the 25 years since it first appeared. Alice first becomes fascinated with and entangled in the drug culture after her family moves from their hometown. She has difficulty adjusting to a new school and making new friends. She is excited by the intensity of the "highs" she experiences on drugs and terrified of the dangers involved.

The book, written in diary form, presents firsthand the life of the West Coast drug culture of the late nineteen sixties–early nineteen seventies. Alice and a friend run away from home, hitchhike from one hippie commune to the next, become prostitutes to support their drug habits, and suffer from disease, degradation, and despair.

After several attempts to free herself from drugs, Alice returns home and receives care and support from her parents, who do everything they can to help her. The book makes clear that overcoming drug addiction involves more than the detoxification process—it means forsaking all your former friends and acquaintances and completely renouncing old habits and hangouts. Although Alice tries to stay straight, she fails to break contact with the "dopers" and is lured back into the vicious cycle of addiction.

The book's strength is its honesty in depicting the allure and the horror of drug addiction and the difficulty in breaking free, not only from the physical addiction to the drugs, but also the emotional and psychological dependence of the drug culture lifestyle. Alice's parents are depicted as loving and caring, wanting beyond everything to help their daughter, and supportive of her efforts to break free. The explicit language, frank descriptions of sexual experiences, and detailed accounts of good and bad "trips" present readers with the consequences of drug addiction and prod them to draw their own conclusions.

The conclusion of the book, in which Alice seems to be making progress in overcoming her problems, is deliberately left open-ended. An epilogue reveals that Alice is found dead of a drug overdose, which may have been accidental, or deliberately administered, or even suicide. This epilogue encourages readers to speculate on Alice's state of mind and to think about what they have just read.

## Challenges

Removed from school libraries in Kalamazoo, Michigan (1974); Levittown, New York (1975); Saginaw, Michigan (1975); Eagle Pass, Texas (1977); Trenton, New Jersey (1977); and North Bergen, New Jersey (1980), due to "objectionable" language and explicit sex scenes.

Challenged at the Marcellus (N.Y.) School District (1975); the Ogden (Utah) School District (1979); and the Safety Harbor, St. Petersburg (Fla.) Middle School Library (1982), where written parental permission was required to check out the title.

Challenged at the Osseo School District in Brooklyn Park, Minnesota (1983), when a school board member found the book's language "personally offensive."

Challenged in the Pagosa Springs (Colo.) schools (1983) because a parent objected to the "graphic language, subject matter, immoral tone, and lack of literary quality found in the book."

Challenged at the Rankin County, Mississippi, School District (1984) because it is "profane and sexually objectionable."

Challenged at the Gwinnett County (Ga.) Middle School (1986) by members of Citizens for Excellence in Education because of "filth, profanities, and perversities." Challenged at the Central Gwinnett (Ga.) High School Library (1986) because "it encourages students to steal and take drugs."

The Gainesville (Ga.) Public Library (1986) prohibits young readers from checking out this book along with 40 other books. The books, on subjects ranging from hypnosis and drug abuse to breast-feeding and sexual dysfunction, are kept in a locked room.

Removed from the middle-school library in Kalkaska, Michigan (1987), because the book contains "objectionable language and encouraged sexual experimentation."

Banned from an English class at Buckhannon-Upshur High School in Buckhannon, West Virginia (1993), following a complaint by two parents about graphic language.

A New York couple asked that the book be removed from a required-reading list for an elective course called "Diaries and Journals" at Johnstown High School (1993) because of the numerous obscenities in two pages. The board of education suggested that school administrators consider the request.

The superintendent of schools in Wall Township, New Jersey (1993), removed copies of the book from the library at the Wall Township Intermediate School because of "inappropriate" language and because it "borders on pornography." He explained that he had originally ordered the book removed from a summer-reading list at the high school, the high school library, all reading lists, and the intermediate school library in 1987; and he was unaware that copies still remained in the schools.

Banned from a ninth-grade reading list at Shepherd Hill High School in Dudley, Massachussetts (1994), more than 25 years after its publication after the police chief, who objected to his daughter reading the book, collected 176 signatures on a petition citing "gross and vulgar language and graphic description of drug use and sexual conduct" and a description of lesbian sex.

## Reviews

*Best Sellers* 32 (Sept. 1, 1972): 263.

*Booklist* 68 (March 15, 1972): 611; 68 (April 1, 1972): 663; 80 (Oct. 15, 1983): 351; 87 (Feb. 1, 1991): 1122; 88 (Feb. 15, 1992): 1100; 91 (Oct. 15, 1994): 413.

*Books and Bookmen* 18 (Jan. 1973): 99.

*Catholic Library World* 43 (Dec. 1971): 219.

*Christian Science Monitor* 63 (Nov. 11, 1971): B6.

*Chronicle of Higher Education* 17 (Feb. 20, 1979): R10.

*Commonweal* 95 (Nov. 19, 1971): 190.

*English Journal* 62 (Jan. 1973): 146.

*High/Low Report* 4 (Oct. 1982): 1.

*Kirkus Reviews* 39 (July 15, 1971): 776.

*Library Journal* 97 (March 15, 1972): 1174; 97 (May 15, 1972): 1884.

*New York Times Book Review,* pt. 2 (Nov. 5, 1972): 42.

*Publishers Weekly* 201 (March 27, 1972): 80.

*Top of the News* 28 (April 1972): 311.

*Times Literary Supplement* (Sept. 1, 1972).

## Articles about This Book

Peck, Richard. "In the Country of Teenage Fiction." *American Libraries* 4 (April 1973): 204–7.

## Awards and Prizes

Best of the Best Books for Young Adults, 1983

Christopher Book Award, 1972

Media and Methods Maxi Award for best paperback, presented by *Media and Methods Magazine,* 1973

Still Alive: Best of the Best Books for Young Adults, 1975

## Sources Recommending This Book

Carter, Betty. *Best Books for Young Adults: The History, the Selections, the Romance.* Chicago: American Library Association, 1994. p. 79.

Kaywell, Joan F. *Adolescents at Risk: A Guide to Fiction and Nonfiction for Young Adults, Parents, and Professionals.* Westport, Conn.: Greenwood, 1993. p. 126.

*Senior High School Library Catalog.* 14th ed. Eds. Brenda Smith and Juliette Yaakov. New York: H. W. Wilson, 1992. p. 246.

Spencer, Pam. *What Do Young Adults Read Next? A Reader's Guide to Fiction for Young Adults.* Detroit: Gale, 1994. p. 503.

*Top One Hundred Countdown: Best of the Best Books for Young Adults,* 1969–1994. Chicago: American Library Association, 1995.

## Audiovisual Resources

*Go Ask Alice.* 16mm film, optical sound. 74 min., color. Distributor: Swank Motion Pictures, Inc., 201 S. Jefferson, St. Louis, MO 63166.

*Go Ask Alice.* 35mm and 16mm, color. Motion picture. 74 min. Producer and distributor: Metromedia Producers Corporation.

*Go Ask Alice.* Made-for-television movie. ABC-TV, 1985. Directed by John Korty and produced by Gerald I. Isenberg.

# The Great Santini

Boston: Houghton Mifflin, 1976

Ben Meacham is a high school senior at the time of the Cuban Missile Crisis when his family moves to yet another duty station with his Marine Corps fighter-pilot father. Ben, as the eldest of four siblings, bears the brunt of his father's temper. His father, Bull Meacham, who refers to himself as the Great Santini, is a racist, a religious hypocrite, a wife and child beater, and totally devoted to the corps. Ben's mother is a very sweet, pious woman who tries to instill high moral values, responsibility, and devotion to her Catholic faith. The entire family suffers under the oppression of never knowing when the Great Santini will explode. Ben is a talented athlete who never measures up to his father's standards and for that he is mercilessly belittled. He struggles through his senior year to reconcile his emerging independence with his father's emphatically enforced expectations.

Although this story is replete with profanity, the powerful message is in the love-hate feelings that Ben, his mother, and his siblings have for Bull. Bull uses emotional manipulation and physical abuse to keep his family off-balance, thereby providing him with the absolute control over their lives that he demands. In the end, the reader is asked to love Bull as his family did, but the author's sensitive portrayal of the personal anguish his family suffered at his hands makes it difficult.

## Challenges

Removed from the Eagan High School classroom in Burnsville, Minnesota (1992).

A 15-year-old sophomore at Guilderland High School in Guilderland, New York (1993), objected to the book, which was assigned to his English class, because he found it offensive and inappropriate for students his age. A district review committee denied his request.

A group of residents in Anaheim, California, requested that the book be banned from the Anaheim Union High School District (1993). The 21-member review committee declined to ban the book. The same group of residents led a recall effort against four members of the school board because they objected to the board's approval of the book, which they described as "vulgar, defiles religion, and is not appropriate for students."

## Reviews

*Booklist* 72 (May 15, 1976): 1320; 87 (Feb. 15, 1991): 1184.

*Commonweal* 118 (Feb. 22, 1991): 128.

*Emergency Librarian* 15 (May 1988): 58.

*Kirkus Reviews* 44 (March 1, 1976): 270.

*Kliatt Paperback Book Guide* 11 (Fall 1977): 4.

*Library Journal* 101 (June 1, 1976): 1307.

*Publishers Weekly* 209 (April 12, 1976): 58; 211 (April 18, 1977): 60.

## Articles about This Book

Rochman, Hazel, and Stephanie Zvirin. "Growing Up Male: Fathers and Sons." *Booklist* 87 (Feb. 15, 1991): 1184.

## Awards and Prizes

Best of the Best Books for Young Adults, 1983

## References about the Author

*Authors and Artists for Young Adults.* Vol. 8. Detroit: Gale, 1992.

*Contemporary Authors, New Revision Series.* Vol. 24. Detroit: Gale, 1984.

*Contemporary Literary Criticism.* Vol. 74. Detroit: Gale, 1993.

*Who's Who in America, 50th ed., 1996.* New Providence, N.J.: Marquis Who's Who, 1995. p. 831.

## Sources Recommending This Book

Gillespie, John T., ed. *Best Books for Senior High Readers.* New Providence, N.J.: R. R. Bowker, 1991. p. 28.

*Growing Up Is Hard to Do.* Ed. Sally Estes. Chicago: Booklist/American Library Association, 1994. p. 12.

## Audiovisual Resources

*The Great Santini.* 16mm film, optical sound. Producer and distributor: Guidance Associates, 90 S. Bedford Road, Mt. Kisco, NY 10549; (800) 431-1242.

# Grendel

New York: Knopf, 1971

John Gardner's *Grendel,* a reworking of the classic epic *Beowulf,* is sometimes challenged because of its unfettered violence and corrupt view of worldly existence. Gardner sets the mood for the story with a segment of poetry from William Blake:

> And if the Babe is born a Boy
> He's given to a Woman Old,
> Who nails him down upon a rock,
> Catches his shrieks in cups of gold.

The reader meets Grendel in the "twelfth year of [his] idiotic life." He describes himself as a "pointless, ridiculous monster crouched in the shadows, stinking of dead men, murdered children, martyred cows. (I am neither proud nor ashamed, understand. One more dull victim, leering at seasons that never were meant to be observed.) 'Ah, sad one, poor old freak!' "

Early in Grendel's youth, he adventures beyond the safety of his mother's cave and becomes trapped in the roots of an ancient oak. While trapped, he sees men for the first time. He understands their language; it is similar to his, although the men cannot understand his peculiar pronunciation. At first the men look at the silent Grendel against the tree and think him a fungus, a growth of some kind.

Then they imagine that this thing may be a spirit. Grendel attempts to speak, and the men become afraid. The king takes an axe and hurls it at Grendel. They fill his body with arrows and javelins until his mother comes to rescue him.

The tragedy of Grendel's life from his point of view and told through his voice allows the reader to see victimization from a different perspective. At once, heros and villains, victims and predators, become confused; there is no black and white. The uncontrolled violence is difficult to fathom, and yet the reader can empathize with the monster. Because of this frame of reference, Grendel is characterized by some as vulgar and profane. It continues to be used, however, in high school classrooms because of Gardner's ability, through this work, to pose metaphysical problems in an ingenious manner.

## Challenges

Complaint filed in the Wasco, California (1987), School District against the book for vulgarity and profanity and because it is "anti-God, anti-religion, and anti-personal dignity."

**53**

In 1991, banned in Kern County, California.

Inclusion in the curriculum challenged in Bass River Township, New Jersey, because of obscenity (1993).

Request for removal of the novel from the school's supplemental reading list by a parent in Jonesboro, Georgia (1993).

## Reviews

*American Literature* 62 (Feb. 1990): 634.

*Atlantic Monthly* 228 (Oct. 1971): 135.

*Booklist* 68 (Dec. 15, 1971): 353.

*Critique* 23 (Aug. 1981): 66.

*Emergency Librarian* 9 (Jan. 1982): 13.

*English Journal* 68 (Feb. 1979): 42; 77 (Dec. 1988): 73; 83 (March 1994): 96.

*Kirkus Reviews* 39 (Aug. 15, 1971): 762.

*Library Journal* 96 (Sept. 1, 1971): 2670; 97 (March 15, 1972): 1180.

*New York Times Book Review* (Sept. 19, 1971): 6.

*Publishers Weekly* 200 (Aug. 19, 1971): 117; 228 (Aug. 30, 1985): 421.

*Saturday Review* 54 (Nov. 27, 1971): 46.

*Time* 98 (Sept. 20, 1971): 89.

*Times Literary Supplement* (July 14, 1972): 793.

*Virginia Quarterly Review* 48 (Winter 1972): 19.

*Voice of Youth Advocates* 8 (Feb. 1986): 410.

## References about the Author

*International Authors and Writers Who's Who.* 9th ed. Ed. Adrian Gaster. Cambridge: International Biographical Centre, 1982.

*Magill's Survey of American Literature.* Ed. Frank N. Magill. North Bellmore, N.Y.: Marshall Cavendish, 1991.

## Sources Recommending This Book

*Fiction Catalog,* 13th ed. Eds. Juliette Yaakov and John Greenfieldt. New York: H. W. Wilson, 1996. p. 243.

Gillespie, John T., ed. *Best Books for Senior High Readers.* New Providence, N.J.: R. R. Bowker, 1991. p. 57.

*The Reader's Advisor: The Best in Reference Works, British Literature & American Literature.* 14th ed. 3 vols. New York: R. R. Bowker, 1994. v. 1, pp. 978–79.

Young Adult Library Services Association. *Outstanding Books for the College Bound: Choices for a Generation.* Chicago: American Library Association, 1996.

*The Young Adult Reader's Adviser.* Vol. 1, *The Best in Literature and Language Arts, Mathematics, and Computer Science.* Ed. Myra Immell. New Providence, N.J.: R. R. Bowker, 1992. p. 6.

## Audiovisual Resources

*Grendel.* 4-track, 1⅞ cassette, 29 min. Producer: New Letters, University of Missouri—Kansas City, 5100 Rockhill Road, Kansas City, MO 64110-2499; (816) 235-1168. Distributor: American Audio Prose Library, P.O. Box 842, Columbia, MO 65205; (800) 447-2275.

*Grendel.* 1-track, 1⅞ cassette. Producer and distributor: Books On Tape, P.O. Box 7900, Newport Beach, CA 92658; (800) 626-3333.

# The Handmaid's Tale

Boston: Houghton Mifflin, 1986

*The Handmaid's Tale,* Margaret Atwood's novel of a frightening future, has often been compared by critics to George Orwell's *1984.* Presented as a taped interview with narrator Offred ("Of Fred"), a Handmaid, the book combines conservative American politics and careless worldwide ecological policies into a future in which women are enslaved and the earth is defiled. Those few remaining women who haven't been rendered sterile by environmental disasters are Handmaids, women whose sole purpose is to be fertilized by high-ranking Commanders, and whose babies are raised by their Wives.

Loss of personal freedom, expression of sex roles, and the earth's environment are themes in this novel. The controversy this novel provokes is rooted in its sexual and religious components. Nearly universally praised by critics when it was published in 1986, *The Handmaid's Tale* contains scenes of the mechanized ménage à trois mating rituals involving Offred, the Commander and his aging, sterile Wife; presents a strong and rebellious lesbian character; and depicts secret sexual liaisons that spring up within the novel's claustrophobic world.

Atwood's satirical, poetic rendering of the official sexual practices in a totalitarian society, based in part on an interpretation of Old Testament scripture, is more frightening than erotic. Offred eventually encounters Moira, her prerevolution lesbian friend, in a brothel patronized by the Commanders, where women are costumed in prerevolution attire—sequined Playboy Bunny outfits, et al. Offred eventually falls in love and has a secret affair with Nick, the Commander's chauffeur. Nick is an Eye (secret police) who may—or may not—smuggle Offred out of Gilead to safety in Canada or England.

Set in a thinly disguised Cambridge, Massachusetts, a current bastion of liberal American thought, the novel depicts bodies of the executed—doctors, professors, "gender traitors" (gay men)—hung on hooks on Harvard Yard's wall. Racism and homophobia run rampant in this theocracy—Jews are deported to Israel, homosexuals are executed, the "Nation of Ham" is resettled in North Dakota. Rumania's anti-birth-control edicts, the religious fanaticism of Iran's government, and colonial New England's Puritan society are some of the recognizable threads in Atwood's dystopia. Yet what has also come to ironic fruition in Atwood's future are feminist principles gone awry—pornography has been outlawed, women no longer wear makeup or clothing with sexual appeal, and accused rapists are torn apart by Handmaids.

Sure to provoke lively discussion among young adults, this novel continues to be widely challenged throughout the United States.

## Challenges

For being too explicit for students, the book was challenged as a book assignment at the Rancho Cotati High School in Rohnert Park, California, in 1990.

Challenged in the Waterloo (Iowa) schools in 1992 because of profanity, lurid passages about sex, and statements defamatory to minorities, God, women, and the disabled.

Removed from the Chicopee (Mass.) High School English class reading list in 1993 because it contains profanity and sex.

## Reviews

*Booklist* 82 (Dec. 1, 1985): 514.

*Canadian Literature* 4 (Fall 1993): 73.

*Choice* 23 (May 1986): 1384; 29 (Oct. 1991): 244; 23 (May 1986): 1384.

*Christian Century* 104 (May 20, 1987): 496.

*Christian Science Monitor* 78 (Feb. 24, 1986): 22.

*Commonweal* 113 (April 25, 1986): 251.

*Emergency Librarian* 16 (Sept. 1988): 54.

*English Journal* 79 (Oct. 1990): 82.

*Fantasy Review* 9 (Sept. 1986): 20.

*Kirkus Reviews* 53 (Dec. 15, 1985): 1333.

*Kliatt Young Adult Paperback Book Guide* 21 (April 1987): 20.

*Locus* 24 (April 1990): 35.

*Library Journal* 111 (Feb. 1, 1986): 91.

*Maclean's* 101 (Oct. 3, 1988): 56.

*Ms.* 15 (Jan 1987): 49.

*Nation* 243 (Dec. 27, 1986): 738.

*Newsweek* 107 (Feb. 17, 1986): 70.

*New York Times* 135 (Jan. 27, 1986): 17.

*New York Times Book Review* 91 (Feb. 9, 1986): 1.

*New Yorker* 62 (May 12, 1986): 118.

*Progressive* 54 (Sept. 1990): 40.

*Publishers Weekly* 228 (Dec. 13, 1985): 45; 231 (Jan. 9, 1987): 51, 87.

*Saturday Night* 101 (Jan. 1986): 39.

*Saturday Review* 12 (June 1986): 74.

*School Librarian* 35 (Aug. 1987): 278.

*Time* 127 (Feb. 10, 1986): 84.

*Voice of Youth Advocates* 9 (Dec. 1986): 212.

*Women's Review of Books* 3 (July 1986): 14.

## Articles about This Book

Benhuniak-Long, Susan. "Feminism and Reproductive Technology." *Choice* 29 (Oct. 1991): 243.

Tait, Sue, and Christy Tyson. "Paperbacks for Young Adults." *Emergency Librarian* 16 (Oct. 1988): 53–54.

## Awards and Prizes

The Booker Prize Shortlist, 1986

Governor General's Award, 1986

The Los Angeles Times Book Prize, 1986

## Sources Recommending This Book

Carter, Betty. *Best Books for Young Adults: The History, the Selections, the Romance.* Chicago: American Library Association, 1994. p. 80.

*Fiction Catalog,* 13th ed. Eds. Juliette Yaakov and John Greenfieldt. New York: H. W. Wilson, 1996. p. 30.

Gillespie, John T., ed. *Best Books for Senior High Readers.* New Providence, N.J.: R. R. Bowker, 1991. p. 119.

Rochman, Hazel. *Against Borders: Promoting Books for a Multicultural World.* Chicago: Booklist/American Library Association, 1993. p. 247.

Spencer, Pam. *What Do Young Adults Read Next? A Reader's Guide to Fiction for Young Adults.* Detroit: Gale, 1994. pp. 20, 136.

*The Young Adult Reader's Adviser. Vol. 1, The Best in Literature and Language Arts, Mathematics, and Computer Science.* Ed. Myra Immell. New Providence, N.J.: R. R. Bowker, 1992. p. 135.

## References about the Author

*Benet's Reader's Encyclopedia,* 3rd ed. New York: Harper, 1987.

Blain, Virginia, Patricia Clements, and Isobel Grundy. *The Feminist Companion to Literature in English.* New Haven, Conn.: Yale University Press, 1990.

*Contemporary Authors, New Revision Series.* Vol. 33. Detroit: Gale, 1991.

*Contemporary Literary Criticism.* Vol. 44. Detroit: Gale, 1987.

*Contemporary Novelists,* 5th ed. Ed. Lesley Henderson. Chicago: St. James, 1991.

*Directory of American Poets and Fiction Writers,* 1991–92 Edition. New York: Poets & Writers, 1990.

*Magill's Survey of World Literature.* Ed. Frank N. Magill. North Bellmore, N.Y.: Marshall Cavendish, 1993.

Reginald, Robert. *Science Fiction and Fantasy Literature, 1975–1991.* Detroit: Gale, 1992.

*Something about the Author.* Vol. 50. Detroit: Gale, 1988.

## Audiovisual Resources

*The Handmaid's Tale*. 4-track, 1⅞ cassette. 12 hours. Distributor: Recorded Books, Inc., 270 Skipjack Road, Prince Frederick, MD 20678; (800) 638-1304.

*The Handmaid's Tale*. Double-track, 1⅞ cassette. "Margaret Atwood Reads from *The Handmaid's Tale*." Series title: Moveable Feast Series. Producer: Moveable Feast. Distributor: American Audio Prose Library, P.O. Box 842, Columbia, MO 65205; (800) 447-2275.

*The Handmaid's Tale*. Motion picture. Cinecom Entertainment Group, 1990.

# I Am the Cheese

New York: Pantheon Books, 1977

Teenager Adam Farmer begins his first-person narrative by describing a bike ride he is taking on a country road in New England. The story beginning innocuously enough, a menacing dialogue is interspersed periodically, appearing to be a conversation between Adam and a psychiatrist/interrogator. Cormier gradually reveals that Adam had questioned oddities in his family and discovered that he has two birth certificates. He confronts his father, who reveals to Adam that his real name is Paul Delmonte, that Mr. Delmonte had been a journalist who had testified in a case connecting organized crime and state government, that the family is in a federal witness protection program, and that the government has relocated the family with new identities.

Shortly after his father reveals Adam/Paul's true identity to him, the family flees to Vermont to avoid trouble from enemies seeking revenge. The family is in a car accident, deliberately caused by an oncoming vehicle. Adam/Paul sees his mother killed and is uncertain of his father's fate. Then Adam/Paul is taken to a confinement facility, where he is kept drugged and is periodically interrogated. He manages to keep a shred of his own will, however.

Cormier's novel portrays the struggle of an individual against a crushing government system. Unwilling to compromise his integrity, Adam/Paul maintains a remnant of self in the face of crushing authoritarian government.

Portraying the U.S. government in such a negative light is at the root of most challenges to *I Am the Cheese*.

## Challenges

Because the novel is "humanistic and destructive of religious and moral beliefs and of national spirit," the book was challenged at the Cornwall (N.Y.) High School in 1985.

Banned from Bay County's four middle schools and three high schools in Panama City, Florida (1986), because of "offensive" language. The controversy escalated on May 7, 1987, when 64 works of literature were banned from classroom teaching, including *The Great Gatsby,* by F. Scott Fitzgerald; *Great Expectations,* by Charles Dickens; *Lord of the Flies,* by William Golding; *The Crucible,* by Arthur Miller; and *The Old Man and the Sea,* by Ernest Hemingway.

## Reviews

*Booklist* 73 (April 1, 1977): 1165; 84 (July 1988): 1829; 87 (Dec. 15, 1990): 828; 87 (Feb. 15, 1991): 1184.

*Book Report* 8 (March 1990): 26.

*Bulletin of the Center for Children's Books* 30 (April 1977): 121.

*Catholic Library World* 49 (Dec. 1977): 198, 234.

*Commonweal* 184 (Nov. 11, 1977): 732.

*English Journal* 67 (Dec. 1978): 83; 72 (Nov. 1983): 59.

*Horn Book* 53 (Aug. 1977): 427; 63 (Jan. 1987): 102.

*Journal of Reading* 25 (May 1982): 777.

*Kirkus Reviews* 45 (April 1, 1977): 363.

*Ms.* 16 (July 1987): 160.

*Newsweek* 90 (Dec. 19, 1977): 85.

*New York Times Book Review* (May 1, 1977): 26; (Nov. 13, 1977): 50; (April 30, 1978): 75.

*Publishers Weekly* 213 (Feb. 13, 1978): 126.

*School Librarian* 40 (Sept. 1992): 85.

*School Library Journal* 23 (May 1977): 35, 78; 36 (Dec. 1990): 39; 38 (Sept. 1992): 158.

*Wilson Library Bulletin* 51 (April 1977): 687.

## Awards and Prizes

Best of the Best Books for Young Adults, 1983

## References about the Author

See listing for *The Chocolate War*.

## Sources Recommending This Book

Carter, Betty. *Best Books for Young Adults: The History, the Selections, the Romance.* Chicago: American Library Association, 1994. pp. 91, 160, 174.

Gillespie, John T., ed. *Best Books for Junior High Readers.* New Providence, N.J.: R. R. Bowker, 1991. p. 48.

Gillespie, John T., ed. *Best Books for Senior High Readers.* New Providence, N.J.: R. R. Bowker, 1991. p. 41.

*Growing Up Is Hard to Do.* Ed. Sally Estes. Chicago: Booklist/American Library Association, 1994. pp. 12, 25, 58.

*Juniorplots 3: A Book Talk Guide for Use with Readers Ages 12–16.* Eds. John T. Gillespie and Corrine J. Nader. New York: R. R. Bowker, 1993.

Rochman, Hazel. *Against Borders: Promoting Books for a Multicultural World.* Chicago: Booklist/American Library Association, 1993. p. 12.

*The Young Adult Reader's Adviser.* Vol. 1, *The Best in Literature and Language Arts, Mathematics, and Computer Science.* Ed. Myra Immell. New Providence, N.J.: R. R. Bowker, 1992. p. 213.

## Audiovisual Resources

*I Am the Cheese.* 4-track, 1⅞ cassette. Producer and distributor: Recorded Books, Inc., 270 Skipjack Road, Prince Frederick, MD 20678; (800) 638-1304.

*I Am the Cheese.* 1-track, 1⅞ cassette. Producer: Miller-Brody Productions, Inc., 2700 Coolidge Ave., Los Angeles, CA 90064. Distributor: Random House, Inc., 400 Hahn Road, Westminster, MD 21157; (800) 726-0600.

# I Know Why the Caged Bird Sings

New York: Random House, 1970

Maya Angelou's first book, the story of her life from the time she arrived in Stamps, Arkansas, at the age of three to the birth of her only child at age sixteen, is moving, eloquent, and a very poignant picture of the life of a young black woman growing up in the middle years of this century. Three-year-old Marguerite (later known as Maya) and her four-year-old brother, Bailey, arrived in Stamps in the early 1920s to live with their father's mother after their parents' divorce. Momma, as they came to call her, raised them as her own for the next ten years. Their mother stayed in the North in order to make money so that she could eventually send for them. Momma and her grown son, Willie, ran a general store in Stamps. Eventually, Marguerite and Bailey left Stamps and moved to St. Louis to live with their mother. The trauma of being raped by her mother's boyfriend, which she recounts in vivid detail, caused Marguerite to lose her speech. She and Bailey moved back to Stamps, where Marguerite was befriended by the aristocratic Mrs. Flowers, who coaxed her back to reality by teaching her the beauty of language in literature. After high school graduation, Marguerite and Bailey moved to California to live with their mother.

Marguerite lived briefly as what we would call a "street person" with a band of homeless children. She survived her experiences and moved back to her mother's home in the Bay Area where she had a baby out-of-wedlock.

*I Know Why the Caged Bird Sings* provides insights into the struggles of a young African American woman in developing personal and cultural identity. Elizabeth Fox-Genovese wrote a scholarly discourse on the book in *Black American Literature Forum* (Summer 1990, pp. 221–35), in which she states that Angelou rejected white norms of womanhood as a model for her own self-development. But she also notes that Angelou had to learn the culture of the dominant society in order to describe and differentiate the expectations of her own culture.

Angelou's style is replete with similes and colorfully descriptive adjectives. Fox-Genovese notes that "[Angelou's] highly crafted, incandescent text selectively explores the intertwining relations of origins and memory to her identity. The unrecognized whiteness of the child she represents herself as having been gives way to the proud blackness of the woman she has become."

## Challenges

A parent at Amador Valley High School in Pleasanton, California (1992), asked that the book be pulled from the required-reading list for sophomores because of sexually explicit language in a scene where Angelou recalls being raped by her mother's boyfriend.

The book was removed from a Banning, California (1992), eighth-grade class after several parents complained about passages involving child molesting and rape.

It was temporarily banned by Lowndes County school administrators in Columbus, Mississippi (1993), from Caledonia Middle School on the grounds "it is too sexually explicit to be read by children."

Parents in Hooks, Texas (1993), requested that the book be removed from the school curriculum. A reconsideration committee voted to retain the book.

Parents in Haines City, Florida (1993), petitioned the Polk County School Board to ban the book from the high school because of the rape scene. The review committee said that the objections to the book were related as much or more to the author's race as to the book's content and declined to ban the book.

Challenged by a parent in Des Moines, Iowa's only Catholic high school (1994) because of inappropriately explicit sexual scenes. The book was retained on the required-reading list for Dowling High School's sophomores.

## Reviews

*American Libraries* 1 (July 1970): 714.

*Booklist* 66 (June 15, 1970): 1256; 66 (July 15, 1970): 1399; 67 (April 1, 1971): 653; 80 (Oct. 15, 1983): 351; 82 (Jan. 1, 1986): 678; 88 (Feb. 15, 1992): 1100; 89 (June 1, 1993): 1864; 91 (Oct. 15, 1994): 412.

*Biography: An Interdisciplinary Quarterly* 15 (Summer 1992): 243.

*Black American Literature Forum* 24 (Summer 1990): 257.

*Black Scholar* 12 (March 1981): 87.

*Choice* 21 (March 1984): 936.

*English Journal* 80 (Dec. 1991): 26.

*Harvard Educational Review* 40 (Nov. 1970): 681.

*Kirkus Reviews* 37 (Dec. 15, 1969): 1330.

*Library Journal* 95 (March 15, 1970): 1018; 95 (June 15, 1970): 2320; 95 (Dec. 15, 1970): 4327.

*Life* 68 (June 5, 1970): 12.

*New Statesman* 107 (Jan. 27, 1984): 26.

*New York Times* 119 (Feb. 25, 1970): 45.

*Newsweek* 75 (March 2, 1970): 89.

*Publishers Weekly* 196 (Dec. 29, 1969): 64; 199 (Jan. 25, 1971): 263.

*Saturday Review* 53 (May 9, 1970): 78.

*School Library Journal* 30 (Jan. 1984): 42; 35 (Oct. 1988): 39; 39 (Feb. 1993): 33.

*Top of the News* 27 (Nov. 1970): 92; 27 (April 1971): 307.

*Wall Street Journal* 175 (April 16, 1970): 16; 176 (Dec. 8, 1970): 22.

## Articles about This Book

Rochman, Hazel. "The Courage of Ordinary Life." *School Library Journal* 30 (Jan. 1984): 42–43.

## Background

Bell, Norman W. "In the Balance: Abusing the Child." *Choice* 21 (March 1984): 931.

## Awards and Prizes

Best Books for Young Adults, 1970

Best of the Best Books for Young Adults, 1983

Best of the Best Books for Young Adults, 1994

Still Alive: The Best of the Best Books for Young Adults, 1975

## References about the Author

*Authors and Artists for Young Adults.* Vol. 7. Detroit: Gale, 1991.

*Benet's Reader's Encyclopedia.* 3rd ed. New York: Harper, 1987.

*Biography Index,* Vol. 17, Sept. 1990–Aug. 1992. New York: Wilson, 1992.

*Black Literature Criticism.* Detroit: Gale, 1992.

*Contemporary Authors, New Revision Series.* Vol. 19. Detroit: Gale, 1987.

*Contemporary Literary Criticism.* Vol. 64. Detroit: Gale, 1991.

*Directory of American Poets and Fiction Writers,* 1991–92 ed. New York: Poets & Writers, 1990.

*Modern American Women Writers.* Eds. Elaine Showalter, Lea Baechler, and A. Walton Litz. New York: Charles Scribner's Sons, 1991.

*Something about the Author.* Vol. 49. Detroit: Gale, 1987.

*Who's Who in America,* 50th ed., 1996. New Providence, N.J.: Marquis Who's Who, 1995. p. 104.

## Sources Recommending This Book

Carter, Betty. *Best Books for Young Adults: The History, the Selections, the Romance.* Chicago: American Library Association, 1994. p. 79.

Gillespie, John T., ed. *Best Books for Senior High Readers.* New Providence, N.J.: R. R. Bowker, 1991. p. 368.

*Growing Up Is Hard to Do.* Ed. Sally Estes. Chicago: Booklist/American Library Association, 1994. pp. 5, 50.

*High-Low Handbook: Encouraging Literacy in the 1990s.* 3rd ed. Comp. and ed. Ellen V. LiBretto. New York: R. R. Bowker, 1990. p. 113.

Miller-Lachman, Lyn. *Our Family, Our Friends, Our World: An Annotated Guide to Significant Multicultural Books for Children and Teenagers.* New Providence, N.J.: R. R. Bowker, 1992. p. 79.

*The Reader's Advisor: The Best in Reference Works, British Literature & American Literature.* 14th ed. 3 vols. New York: R. R. Bowker, 1994. v. 1, pp. 934–35.

Rochman, Hazel. *Against Borders: Promoting Books for a Multicultural World.* Chicago: Booklist/American Library Association, 1993. pp. 104, 130, 162.

Young Adult Library Services Association. *Outstanding Books for the College Bound: Choices for a Generation.* Chicago: American Library Association, 1996.

*The Young Adult Reader's Adviser.* Vol. 1, *The Best in Literature and Language Arts, Mathematics, and Computer Science.* Ed. Myra Immell. New Providence, N.J.: R. R. Bowker, 1992. pp. 190–91.

## Audiovisual Resources

*I Know Why the Caged Bird Sings.* 4-track, 1⅞ cassette. 179 min. Producer: Random House. Distributor: American Audio Prose Library, P.O. Box 842, Columbia, MO 65205; (800) 447-2275. Same format also distributed by Audio Editions, P.O. Box 7930, Auburn, CA 95604; and Random House, 400 Hahn Road, Westminster, MD 21157; (800) 726-0600.

*I Know Why the Caged Bird Sings.* 35mm filmstrip, cassette. Producer and distributor: Current Affairs Films, Div. of Key Productions, 346 Ethan Allen Hwy., Route 7, P.O. Box 426, Ridgefield, CT 06877; (203) 431-0421.

*I Know Why the Caged Bird Sings.* 16mm film, color, no additional information; 3/4- or 1/2-inch video. Distributor: Learning Corporation of America, 108 Wilmot Road, Deerfield, IL 60015; (800) 621-2131.

*I Know Why the Caged Bird Sings.* CBS-TV, 1979.

# Lord of the Flies

London: Faber & Faber, 1954

When the plane evacuating them from their school is shot down by enemy fire and crashes, a group of young boys is stranded on an uninhabited island. All of the adults on board are killed in the crash, and the boys are left to fend for themselves. The older boys propose to elect a leader and establish a fair system for gathering food, building shelters, and maintaining a signal fire to attract rescuers. They have every intention of behaving like reasonable men, imitating adults by discussing and voting on all their decisions as a group.

But these efforts to maintain order break down as fear of the unknown brings more primitive instincts to the surface. One of the strongest and most daring boys challenges the organization of the leaders. The group reverts to a mob, with the strongest boy imposing his will on the others. They obey out of fear and admiration of his prowess. The new "chief" sets up an idol, or totem, of a pig's head, which will magically protect them from their secret terrors as long as they obey it. He acts as spokesman and interpreter of the pig's commands. These commands become more and more irrational and savage, until the mob, under the chief's command, begins hunting down and killing the former leaders.

The last of these is saved from a brutal death only when a passing ship sees the smoke of the fires set to flush him out of hiding and sends a boat ashore to investigate. The savage hunters revert to obedient school boys as soon as adult authority is reimposed.

The author implies, however, that the adults have only managed to disguise their own savagery, as the rescue ship turns out to be a navy destroyer on a mission to hunt down enemy ships.

Golding examines the nature of man and what constitutes civilized (redeemed) as opposed to savage (unredeemed) behavior. Some critics have interpreted Golding's fable as an attempt to show that man in his natural state, depending on his reason alone, cannot achieve a state of grace or salvation. His flawed nature will always bring him low. Only the intervention of God's saving grace can bring about redemption for the world.

In its style and substance, *Lord of the Flies* is remarkably like both Greek tragedy and the biblical parable. Perhaps this accounts for the disquieting sensations that the book creates in its readers, who may not be prepared to discover either Aristotle's catharsis or the lost Garden of Eden lurking beneath the trappings of a laconic adventure story.

Images and symbols are used with deliberate but ambiguous intent. Nothing is what it first seems, and the story is open-ended: The readers must decide for themselves what lurks beneath the surface of society.

## Challenges

Challenged at the Dallas (Tex.) Independent School District high school libraries (1974).

Challenged at the Sully Buttes (S.D.) High School (1981).

Challenged at the Owen (N.C.) High School (1981) because the book is "demoralizing, inasmuch as it implies that man is little more than an animal."

Challenged at the Marana (Ariz.) High School (1983) as an inappropriate reading assignment.

Challenged at the Olney (Tex.) Independent School District (1984) because of "excessive violence and bad language."

Challenged as optional reading for a tenth-grade English class in Lincoln, Nebraska (1987), for its "portrayal of human nature, cruelty and violence, and because it does not represent the values of the home."

Challenged in the Waterloo (Iowa) schools, in 1992, because of profanity, lurid passages about sex, and statements defamatory to minorities, God, women, and the disabled.

## Reviews

*Booklist* 81 (July 1985): 1546; 85 (Oct. 1, 1988): 261; 90 (Dec. 1, 1993): 334.

*Library Journal* 80 (Sept. 1, 1955): 1815.

*New Statesman* 48 (Sept. 25, 1954): 370.

*New York Times Book Review* (Oct. 23, 1955): 38.

*Saturday Review* 38 (Oct. 15, 1955): 16.

*Times Literary Supplement* (Oct. 22, 1954): 669.

*Wilson Library Bulletin* 69 (Dec. 1994): 39.

## Articles about this Book

Baker, James R. "Interview with William Golding." *Twentieth-Century Literature* 28 (Summer 1982): 109–29.

Barr, Donald. "Should Holden Caulfield Read These Books?" *New York Times Book Review* 91 (May 4, 1986): 1, 50–51.

Bien, P. "Vision of a Latter Day Modernist: William Golding's Nobel Prize." *World Literature Today* 58 (Spring 1984): 185–88.

Egan, John M. "Golding's View of Man." *America* 108 (Jan. 26, 1963): 140–41.

Green, M. "Distaste for the Contemporary." *Nation* 190 (May 21, 1960): 451–54.

Hynes, Samuel. "Novels of a Religious Man." *Commonweal* 71 (March 18, 1960): 673–75.

Jones, R. "William Golding: Genius and Sublime Silly-Billy." *Virginia Quarterly Review* 60 (Autumn 1984): 675–87.

Peter, John. "The Fables of William Golding." *Kenyon Review* 19 (Autumn 1957): 577–92.

Purvin, G. "*Lord of the Flies*—Revisited." *Humanist* 44 (July–Aug. 1984): 31.

Rexroth, Kenneth. "William Golding." *Atlantic Monthly* 215 (May 1965): 96–98.

Selby, K. "Golding's *Lord of the Flies*." *Explicator* 41 (Spring 1983): 57–59.

## Background

Baker, James R. *William Golding: A Critical Study*. New York: St. Martin's, 1965.

*Casebook Edition of William Golding's* Lord of the Flies—*Text, Notes and Criticism*. Eds. James R. Baker and Arthur B. Siegler Jr. New York: Putnam, 1964.

Dick, Bernard F. "The Anarchy Within" and "Epilogue." In *William Golding*. New York: Twayne, 1967. pp. 18–36; 96–104.

Epstein, E. L. "Notes on *Lord of the Flies;* Epilogue to *Lord of the Flies* by William Golding." In *Praise from Famous Men: An Anthology of Introductions*. Ed. Guy R. Lyle. Metuchen, N.J.: Scarecrow, 1977. pp. 69–74.

Golding, William. "Fable." In *The Hot Gates and Other Occasional Pieces*. New York: Harcourt, 1966. pp. 85–101.

Golding, William. "A Moving Target" and "Utopias and Antiutopias." In *A Moving Target*. New York: Farrar, 1982. pp. 154–70; 171–84.

Hynes, Samuel. *William Golding*. New York: Columbia University Press, 1964.

Johnston, Arnold. *Of Earth and Darkness: The Novels of William Golding*. Columbia, Mo.: University of Missouri Press, 1980.

Kermode, Frank. *Puzzles and Epiphanies*. London: Routledge & Kegan Paul; New York: Chilmark Press, 1962. pp. 198–218.

Oldsey, Bernard S., and Stanley Weintraub. *The Art of William Golding*. New York: Harcourt, Brace & World, 1965.

Richter, D. H. "Allegory Versus Fable: Golding's *Lord of the Flies*." In *Fable's End: Completeness and Closure in Rhetorical Fiction*. Chicago: University of Chicago Press, 1974. pp. 61–82.

*Talk: Conversations with William Golding*. Jack I. Biles and William Golding. New York: Harcourt, Brace & World, 1970.

*William Golding: Some Critical Considerations*. Eds. Jack I. Biles and Robert O. Evans. Lexington, Ky.: University Press of Kentucky, 1978.

Woodward, Kathleen M. "On Aggression: William Golding's *Lord of the Flies*." In *No Place Else: Explorations in Utopian and Dystopian Fiction*. Edited by Eric S.

Rabkin, Martin H. Greenberg, and Joseph D. Olander. Carbondale, Ill.: Southern Illinois University Press, 1983. pp. 199–224.

## Awards and Prizes

Nobel Prize for Literature, for the body of William Golding's work, 1983

## References about the Author

*Contemporary Authors, New Revision Series*. Detroit: Gale, 1984. v. 13, pp. 219–26.

*Contemporary Literary Criticism*. Detroit: Gale, dates vary. v. 1, pp. 119–22; v. 2, pp. 165–69; v. 3, pp. 196–201; v. 8, pp. 249–50; v. 17, pp. 157–81; v. 27 pp. 159–70.

*Contemporary Novelists*. 4th ed. New York: St. Martin's, 1986. pp. 351–53.

*Encyclopedia of World Literature in the Twentieth Century*. rev. ed. 4 vols. New York: Ungar, 1982. v. 2, pp. 251–52.

## Sources Recommending This Book

*Fiction Catalog*. 13th ed. Eds. Juliette Yaakov and John Greenfieldt. New York. H. W. Wilson, 1996. p. 259.

*Fiction for Youth: A Guide to Recommended Books*. 2nd ed. Ed. Lillian L. Shapiro. New York: Neal-Schuman, 1986. p. 75.

Gillespie, John T., ed. *Best Books for Senior High Readers*. New Providence, N.J.: R. R. Bowker, 1991. p. 8.

*Growing Up Is Hard to Do*. Ed. Sally Estes. Chicago: Booklist/American Library Association, 1994. pp. 25, 58.

*Junior High School Library Catalog*. 6th ed. Eds. Gary L. Bodart and Richard H. Isaacson. New York: H. W. Wilson, 1990. p. 362.

*The Reader's Advisor: The Best in Reference Works, British Literature & American Literature*. 14th ed. 3 vols. New York: R. R. Bowker, 1994. v. 1, p. 483.

*Senior High School Library Catalog*. 14th ed. New York: H. W. Wilson, 1992. p. 686.

Spencer, Pam. *What Do Young Adults Read Next? A Reader's Guide to Fiction for Young Adults*. Detroit: Gale, 1994. pp. 6, 587.

Young Adult Library Services Association. *Outstanding Books for the College Bound: Choices for a Generation*. Chicago: American Library Association, 1996.

*The Young Adult Reader's Adviser*. Vol. 1, *The Best in Literature and Language Arts, Mathematics, and Computer Science*. Ed. Myra Immell. New Providence, N.J.: R. R. Bowker, 1992. p. 89.

## Audiovisual Resources

*Lord of the Flies.* 1/2-inch videocassette. 91 min. Producer and distributor: Guidance Associates, 90 South Bedford Road, Mt. Kisco, NY 10549; (800) 431-1242.

*Lord of the Flies.* 1/2-inch videocassette. 17 min. Series title: Nobel Prize Series—Literature. Distributor: Sunburst Communications, 39 Washington Ave., Room SK16, Pleasantville, NY 10570-3498; (800) 431-1934.

*Lord of the Flies.* Double-track, 1⅞ cassette. "William Golding Reads *Lord of the Flies.*" Producer: Listening Library, Inc., 1 Park Ave., Old Greenwich, CT 06870; (203) 637-3666. Distributor: American Audio Prose Library, P.O. Box 842, Columbia, MO 65205; (800) 447-2275. Unabridged. Six cassettes.

# Of Mice and Men

New York: Covici Friede, 1937

*Of Mice and Men* is the story of the friendship between two itinerant California laborers, George and Lennie. George protects Lennie, a large and powerful but mentally disabled man, from the harassment and cruel teasing of those who are too ignorant to know better. George and Lennie's dream is to find a place of their own where they can live in peace and dignity, but this dream is shattered by Lennie's innocent violence. The story ends when George must kill Lennie to save him from an ignoble death at the hands of a lynch mob led by the husband of a woman Lennie killed unintentionally.

Steinbeck's short novel is considered an American classic. It has been a standard on high school required-reading lists for several generations. The play was voted the best of the 1938 season by the New York Drama Critics Circle. A 1939 film version was similarly praised, and retains its luster even today. In 1981 the play was redone for television and again won critical acclaim.

Its value for high school students lies not only in its sensitive portrayal of innocence betrayed, but in its eloquent brevity, the biblical origins of its themes, and its emotional power. Two main elements of the story, the mentally disabled protagonist and the violence of the action, have proven to be controversial. Yet for these very reasons, the book lends itself to vigorous critical discussion.

*Of Mice and Men* is particularly appropriate to stimulate an examination of such issues as personal responsibility, the nature and obligations of friendship, and the biblical question, Am I my brother's keeper?

## Challenges

Challenged in the Riviera (Tex.) schools (1990); in Buckingham County, Virginia, schools (1991); and by a school board member in Rapides Parish, Louisiana (1993), because it contains profanity.

Attempts were made to remove it from the curriculum at Ringgold High School, Carroll Township, Pennsylvania (1991), because of terminology offensive to blacks.

A petition containing more than one thousand names objecting to the novel was presented to the Campbell County School Board, Jacksboro, Tennessee (1991), citing "blasphemous language, excessive cursing, and sexual overtones."

One parent challenged the inclusion of the book on a required-reading list for tenth-grade students in Buckingham County, Virginia (1992), because "(W)e have promised God that we would raise our child in a Christian home. This goes completely against what we have promised God." A review committee studied the complaint and concluded that parents could restrict their own children's reading, but that the book would be retained on reading lists.

A group from Alba High School in Bayou La Batre, Alabama (1992), called on the school board to create a committee to study parental concerns about "obscene" material and focused on Steinbeck's book as "mentally, emotionally, psychologically and spiritually harmful to children."

In 1992, it was included on a growing list of books held in the back rooms of Duval County (Fla.) public school libraries, requiring parental permission, because parents complained that the books are inappropriate.

Challenged by a parent in Hamilton, Ohio (1992), because of vulgarity and racial slurs. "Parents and Christians are angry over the cuss words in this book," he said. After review by an ad-hoc committee of parents and community members, the book was returned to the recommended-reading list.

Challenged as part of a textbook purchase in Waterloo, Iowa (1992), because of what some said were profanity and statements defamatory to minorities, God, women, and the disabled. The board recommended purchase of the books.

Challenged in Modesto, California (1992), because it contains the word *nigger*. The request to remove it from school reading lists was turned down by school officials. It was appealed to the school board.

Challenged in Alexandria, Louisiana (1992), by a school board member "because of its use of profanity." The school board declined to ban the book.

Challenged formally in Mingus, Arizona (1993), by a parent as an inappropriate assignment in the Mingus Union High School English curriculum because of its "allegedly profane language, moral statement, treatment of the retarded, and violent ending."

Challenged by the father of two Keene Middle School students in Keene, New Hampshire (1993), because of some of the language and subject matter in the book. The parent said, "This language is offensive to me as a born-again Christian."

Pulled from a classroom by a Putnam County (Tenn.) school superintendent (1994), who stated that "due to the language in it, we just can't have this kind of book being taught."

Challenged at the Loganville (Ga.) High School (1994) because of its "vulgar language throughout."

## Reviews

*Booklist* 33 (May 1939): 276.

*Manchester Guardian* (Sept. 14, 1937): 4.

*Nation* 144 (March 6, 1937): 275.

*New Republic* 90 (March 3, 1937): 118.

*New York Times* (Jan. 23, 1937): 20.

*North American Review* 243 (June 1937): 406–13.

*Saturday Review of Literature* 15 (Feb. 27, 1937): 7.

*School Library Journal* 26 (Aug. 1980): 44.

*Studies in Short Fiction* 31 (Fall 1994): 595.

*Western American Literature* 29 (Winter 1995): 291.

*Wilson Library Bulletin* 33 (May 1937): 100.

*Yale Review* 26 (Summer 1937): vi.

## Background

Benson, Jackson J. *The True Adventures of John Steinbeck, Writer: A Biography*. New York: Viking, 1984.

French, Warren. "John Steinbeck." In *Fifteen Modern American Authors: A Survey of Research and Criticism*. Ed. Jackson R. Bryer. Durham, N.C.: Duke University Press, 1969. pp. 369–87.

French, Warren. "John Steinbeck." In *Sixteen Modern American Authors, Volume Two: A Survey of Research and Criticism Since 1972*. Ed. Jackson R. Bryer. Durham, N.C.: Duke University Press, 1990. pp. 582–622.

Goldhurst, William. "*Of Mice and Men*: John Steinbeck's Parable of the Curse of Cain." *Western American Literature* 4, no. 2 (Summer 1971): pp. 123–35.

Jain, Sunita. *John Steinbeck's Concept of Man: A Critical Study of His Novels*. New Delhi: New Statesman Publishing, 1979; Atlantic Highlands, N.J.: Humanities, 1980.

Levant, Howard. *The Novels of John Steinbeck: A Critical Study*. Columbia, Mo.: University of Missouri Press, 1975.

Owens, Leslie. "*Of Mice and Men*: The Dreams of Commitment." In *Modern Critical Views: John Steinbeck*. Ed. Harold Bloom. New York: Chelsea House, 1987. pp. 145–49.

*Steinbeck: A Collection of Critical Essays*. Ed. Robert M. Davis. Englewood Cliffs, N.J.: Prentice-Hall, 1972.

## Awards and Prizes

Best of the Century (poll) in *Writer's Digest*, December 1990, p. 36

Best Play, New York Drama Critics Circle Award, 1938

Nobel Prize for Literature, for the body of John Steinbeck's work, 1962

## References about the Author

*Contemporary Literary Criticism*. Detroit: Gale, 1976. v. 5, pp. 406–409; v. 21, pp. 366, 372, 378–86, 389–92; v. 75, pp. 334–66; v. 75, pp. 334–66.

*Dictionary of Literary Biography*. Vol. 7: *Twentieth-Century American Dramatists, Part 2: K-Z*. Ed. John MacNicholas. Detroit: Gale, 1981. pp. 271–76.

*1300 Critical Evaluations of Selected Novels and Plays.* Ed. Frank Magill. Englewood Cliffs, N.J.: Salem, 1976. v. 3, p. 1606.

## Sources Recommending This Book

*Fiction Catalog.* 13th ed. Eds. Julie Yaakov and John Greenfieldt. New York: H. W. Wilson. 1996. p. 621.

*Fiction for Youth: A Guide to Recommended Books.* 2nd ed. Ed. Lillian Shapiro. New York: Neal-Schuman, 1986. pp. 182–83.

Gillespie, John T., ed. *Best Books for Senior High Readers.* New Providence, N.J.: R. R. Bowker, 1991. p. 82.

*The Reader's Advisor: The Best in Reference Works, British Literature & American Literature.* 14th ed. 3 vols. New York: R. R. Bowker, 1994. v. 1, pp. 883–84.

*Senior High School Library Catalog.* 14th ed. Eds. Brenda Smith and Juliette Yaakov. New York: H. W. Wilson, 1992. p. 719.

Spencer, Pam. *What Do Young Adults Read Next? A Reader's Guide to Fiction for Young Adults.* Detroit: Gale, 1994, p. 392.

Young Adult Library Services Association. *Outstanding Books for the College Bound: Choices for a Generation.* Chicago: American Library Association, 1996.

*The Young Adult Reader's Adviser.* Vol. 1, *The Best in Literature and Language Arts, Mathematics, and Computer Science.* Ed. Myra Immell. New Providence, N.J.: R. R. Bowker, 1992. pp. 288–89.

## Audiovisual Resources

*Of Mice and Men.* 4-track, $1\frac{7}{8}$ cassette. Producer and distributor: Recorded Books, Inc., 270 Skipjack Road, Prince Frederick, MD 20678; (800) 638-1304.

*Of Mice and Men.* Motion picture. MGM Pictures, 1992.

*Of Mice and Men.* Play produced for television in 1981. Director: Reza Badiyi.

S. E. HINTON

# The Outsiders

New York: Viking Press, 1966

Ponyboy Curtis, age 14, is the youngest of three brothers, surviving in a home without parents. Sodapop, age 16, has quit school to work in a gas station; and Darryl (Darry) works two jobs to support the family. Ponyboy gives a realistic and poignant account of what it feels like to grow up on the wrong side of the tracks, in constant conflict with society and its rules. On a more personal level, he describes the "soc's," monied kids who have it all and prey on the "greasers" for fun.

Ponyboy relates, in a direct and honest way, the sense of loyalty and commitment that he and his gang have for each other. There is an underlying caring among these street-hardened toughs who recognize that whatever society may think of them, they can turn to their own gang to provide the security, belonging, and acceptance that is lacking in other areas of their lives. Coming from a broken home, being unable to afford nice clothes, or not living in a decent house—none of this matters. Acceptance is granted because of who you are, not what you have.

Violence is a natural part of Ponyboy's way of life, and is integral to the story. Most of his friends carry switchblades and are not afraid to use them. Survival is basic—being ready to jump and stab someone else before he has a chance to hurt you is simply a way to stay alive. Yet the characters also show a naive idealism about the future—the grim reality of their daily lives does not prevent them from dreaming about better lives and imagining how things might be different.

Inevitably, the violence causes tragedy, when Ponyboy and Johnny are attacked by the "soc's" and Johnny ends up stabbing and killing one of them in self-defense. This action indirectly causes the death of Dallas, the toughest of the toughs, who is injured while attempting to rescue a child from the burning church where Ponyboy has been hiding.

*The Outsiders* is generally viewed as a ground-breaking book in the field of young adult fiction. Many people credit Hinton with beginning a new tradition in writing for teens—away from the sugar-coated, conflict-free books of the late fifties and early sixties and toward an intensely experienced realism. Because *The Outsiders* created a new concept in writing for teens, it also sparked controversy. People objected to the realism, arguing that teenagers were not ready for such a realistic portrayal of the world. Other objections were to the characters' life-styles, which included smoking, drinking, lacking respect for authority, and lacking parenting.

After 25 years and millions of readers, *The Outsiders* remains a classic of young adult literature.

## Challenges

Banned from classroom use in Panama City, Florida (1987), by a school superintendent for "profanity" and "a lot of vulgar language."

Challenged in Milwaukee, Wisconsin (1987), for being "too negative," for portraying drug and alcohol abuse, and for depicting characters from broken homes.

In 1992, a complaint was filed in the Boone (Iowa) School District against both the book and the video for glamorizing smoking and drinking and because "violence and the use of obscenities are also excessive in the book."

## Reviews

*Best Sellers* 27 (Dec. 1967): 144.

*Book Week* 4 (June 18, 1967): 14.

*Booklist* 64 (Oct. 1, 1967): 176; 91 (June 1, 1995): 1760.

*Bulletin of the Center for Children's Books* 20 (July–Aug. 1967): 171.

*English Journal* 81 (Nov. 1992): 57.

*Horn Book* 43 (Aug. 1967): 475.

*Journal of Reading* 22 (Nov. 1978): 126.

*Kirkus Reviews* 35 (April 15, 1967): 506.

*Library Journal* 92 (May 15, 1967): 2028.

*New York Times Book Review* 72, pt. 2 (May 7, 1967): 10.

*Publishers Weekly* 191 (May 22, 1967): 64.

*Saturday Review* 50 (May 13, 1967): 59.

*School Library Journal* 36 (Dec. 1990): 39.

*Wilson Library Bulletin* 60 (Sept. 1985): 63.

## Articles about This Book

"The Novels of S. E. Hinton: Springboard to Personal Growth for Adolescents." *Adolescence* 22 (Fall 1987): 642–46.

Seay, Ellen A. "Opulence to Decadence: *The Outsiders* and *Less than Zero*." *English Journal* 76 (Oct. 1987): 69–72.

## Background

Daly, Jay. *Presenting S. E. Hinton*. Boston: Twayne, 1987.

Farber, Stephen. "Directors Join the S. E. Hinton Fan Club." *New York Times* (March 3, 1983): 2, 19.

Peck, Richard. "In the Country of Teenage Fiction." *American Libraries* 4 (April 1973): 204–7.

Robin, Lisa. "S. E. Hinton Knows How to Write for the Young and the Restless." *Media and Methods* 18 (June–July 1982): 28.

Stanek, Lou Willett. "Real People, Real Books: About YA Readers." *Top of the News* 31 (June 1975): 417–27.

Sutherland, Zena. "Books for Young People." *Saturday Review* 50 (May 13, 1967): 59.

## Awards and Prizes

Margaret A. Edwards Award (then entitled the *School Library Journal* Young Adult Author Award), presented for the body of Hinton's work by the Young Adult Library Services Association of the American Library Association, 1988

Massachusetts Children's Book Award, 1979

Media and Methods Maxi Award for best paperback, presented by *Media and Methods Magazine,* 1975

Nothin' But the Best: Best of the Best Books for Young Adults, 1988

Still Alive: The Best of the Best Books for Young Adults, 1975

## References about the Author

*Children's Literature Review.* Detroit: Gale, 1978. v. 3, p. 69.

*Something about the Author.* Detroit: Gale, 1980. v. 19, pp. 147–48; v. 58, pp. 96–106.

## Sources Recommending This Book

Anderson, Vicki. *Fiction Index for Readers 10 to 16.* Jefferson, N.C.: McFarland, 1992.

Carter, Betty. *Best Books for Young Adults: The History, the Selections, the Romance.* Chicago: American Library Association, 1994. pp. 39, 69, 173, 175.

Gillespie, John T., ed. *Best Books for Junior High Readers.* New Providence, N.J.: R. R. Bowker, 1991. p. 6.

*Growing Up Is Hard to Do.* Ed. Sally Estes. Chicago: Booklist/American Library Association, 1994. pp. 56, 59.

*High-Low Handbook: Encouraging Literacy in the 1990s.* 3rd ed. Comp. and ed. Ellen V. LiBretto. New York: R. R. Bowker, 1990. p. 243.

*Junior High School Library Catalog.* 6th ed. Ed. Juliette Yaakov. New York: H. W. Wilson, 1990.

Kaywell, Joan F. *Adolescents at Risk: A Guide to Fiction and Nonfiction for Young Adults, Parents and Professionals.* Westport, Conn.: Greenwood, 1993. p. 167.

*Nothin' But the Best.* Chicago: American Library Association, 1988.

*Senior High School Library Catalog.* 14th ed. Eds. Brenda Smith and Juliette Yaakov. New York: H. W. Wilson, 1992.

Spencer, Pam. *What Do Young Adults Read Next? A Reader's Guide to Fiction for Young Adults.* Detroit: Gale, 1994. pp. 225, 376.

*Top One Hundred Countdown: Best of the Best Books for Young Adults, 1969–1994.* Chicago: American Library Association: 1995.

*The Young Adult Reader's Adviser.* Vol. 1, *The Best in Literature and Language Arts, Mathematics, and Computer Science.* Ed. Myra Immell. New Providence, N.J.: R. R. Bowker, 1992. pp. 239–40.

*Your Reading: A Booklist for Junior High and Middle School Students.* 9th ed. Urbana, Ill.: National Council of Teachers of English, 1993.

## Audiovisual Resources

*The Outsiders.* Motion picture. Producer: Zoetrop, 1983.

*The Outsiders.* Videodisc. Producer and distributor: Barr Films, 12801 Schabarum Ave., P.O. Box 7878, Irwindale, CA 91706-7878; (800) 234-7878.

*The Outsiders.* 4-track, $1\frac{7}{8}$ cassette. Producer and distributor: Audio Editions, P.O. Box 6930, Auburn, CA 95604; (800) 231-4261.

*The Outsiders.* 4-track, $1\frac{7}{8}$ cassette. Producer: Listening Library, Inc., 1 Park Ave., Old Greenwich, CT 06870; (203) 637-3666. Distributor: G. K. Hall Audio, 70 Lincoln St., Boston, MA 02111; (800) 343-2806.

*The Outsiders.* 1-track, $1\frac{7}{8}$ cassette. 29 min. Producer: Center for Cassette Studies, Inc., 8110 Webb Ave., North Hollywood, CA 91605; (213) 875-1265.

*The Outsiders.* 1-track, $1\frac{7}{8}$ cassette. Producer: Miller-Brody Productions, Inc., 2700 Coolidge Ave., Los Angeles, CA 90064; (213) 478-3379. Distributor: Random House, Inc., 400 Hahn Road, Westminster, MD 21157; (800) 726-0600.

*The Outsiders.* 3/4- or 1/2-inch videocassette. Producer and distributor: Guidance Associates, 90 South Bedford Road, Mt. Kisco, NY 10549; (800) 431-1242.

*The Outsiders.* 3/4- or 1/2-inch videocassette. Distributor: Center for Humanities, Communications Park, Box 1000, Mt. Kisco, NY 10549-0101.

# Running Loose

New York: Greenwillow Books, 1983

During Louie Banks's senior year of high school, two events—and Louie's responses to them—change his entire life. A good athlete, Louie is a starter on his small Idaho high school's football team. During a critical game, his coach instructs the team to play unfairly, resulting in the injury of the opposing team's star athlete, an African American, who sustains a few broken ribs. The racism in his community, as well as his coach's unethical behavior, forces Louie to take a public stand against the coach; and the coach kicks Louie off the team.

Soon after this fateful game, Louie suffers a much more serious loss. His girlfriend, Becky, is killed in a car accident; and again, Louie's ethics appear to conflict with those of his community. In a grief-stricken outburst at Becky's funeral, Louie loudly chides the minister, who did not know Becky, for a phony sermon. Later, Louie takes a sledgehammer to the memorial plaque that the principal installs for Becky.

Crutcher uses a young man's maturational process to tell a story about his reaction to a community's hypocrisy. Crutcher portrays the sexual intimacy between Louie and Becky without explicit detail, confronts racism (including the use of an offensive ra-cial epithet), and tells of a coach willing to break all the rules for the sake of winning.

The book nicely dovetails a critical adolescent milestone, that of defining one's identity and finding one's role in the human community, tasks that Louie manages with the support of loving parents, an assistant coach, and an understanding employer.

## Challenges

Challenged at the Gwinnett County (Ga.) public schools in 1986 because of its discussion of sex.

## Reviews

*Booklist* 79 (April 1, 1983): 1019; 86 (May 1, 1990): 1696; 87 (Feb. 15, 1991): 1184.

*Bulletin of the Center for Children's Books* 36 (May 1983): 165.

*Emergency Librarian* 14 (Sept. 1986): 22; 18 (Jan. 1991): 71.

*English Journal* 73 (Dec. 1984): 64; 77 (April 1988): 84; 81 (March 1992): 82.

*Horn Book* 59 (Aug. 1983): 451; 64 (May 1988): 332.

*Journal of Reading* 27 (Nov. 1983): 183.

*Kirkus Reviews* 51 (April 15, 1983): 461.

*Kliatt Young Adult Paperback Book Guide* 20 (Spring 1986): 6.

*Publishers Weekly* 223 (April 1, 1983): 60; 229 (March 21, 1986): 93.

*School Library Journal* 29 (May 1983): 80; 35 (Oct. 1988): 40.

*Voice of Youth Advocates* 6 (April 1983): 36; 14 (Feb. 1992): 359.

## Awards and Prizes

Nothin' But the Best: Best of the Best Books for Young Adults, 1988

## References about the Author

*Authors and Artists for Young Adults.* Vol. 9. Detroit: Gale, 1992.

*Children's Literature Review.* Vol. 28. Detroit: Gale, 1992.

*Contemporary Authors, New Revision Series,* Vol. 36. Detroit: Gale, 1992.

## Sources Recommending This Book

Carter, Betty. *Best Books for Young Adults: The History, the Selections, the Romance.* Chicago: American Library Association, 1994. pp. 93, 163, 175.

Gillespie, John T., ed. *Best Books for Junior High Readers.* New Providence, N.J.: R. R. Bowker, 1991. p. 119.

*Growing Up Is Hard to Do.* Ed. Sally Estes. Chicago: Booklist/American Library Association, 1994. p. 13.

*Juniorplots 4: A Book Talk Guide for Use with Readers Ages 12–16.* Eds. John T. Gillespie and Corrine J. Nader. New York: R. R. Bowker, 1993. p. 276.

Kaywell, Joan F. *Adolescents at Risk: A Guide to Fiction and Nonfiction for Young Adults, Parents and Professionals.* Westport, Conn.: Greenwood, 1993. pp. 19, 209.

Spencer, Pam. *What Do Young Adults Read Next? A Reader's Guide to Fiction for Young Adults.* Detroit: Gale, 1994. pp. 89, 120, 282, 334, 492, 547.

# Slaughterhouse-Five; or, The Children's Crusade

New York: Delacorte Press, 1969

*Slaughterhouse-Five* raises disturbing questions of morality versus power. The main protagonist, Billy Pilgrim, optometrist and World War II veteran, takes us on a "trip" to Dresden during the war and to the alien planet of Tralfamadore.

We learn that Billy has suffered a breakdown and has been hospitalized by his daughter. He is kidnapped and transported to Tralfamadore, where he is mated with Montana Wildhack. The trip to Tralfamadore is Billy's escape from the horrors he witnessed during the Dresden bombing.

The struggle of conscience to reconcile the horrors carried out in the course of waging war with the principles the war is ostensibly fought to defend, is revealed in this antiwar novel of the nineteen seventies. "So it goes" is the call sign of our hero throughout this laid-back satire.

## Challenges

Banned in Rochester, Michigan (1972), because the novel "contains and makes references to religious matters" and thus fell within the establishment clause.

An appellate court upheld its usage in the school in *Todd v Rochester Community Schools,* 41 Mich App 320, 200 NW2d 90 (1972).

Challenged in many communities, but burned in Drake, North Dakota (1973). After the burning of the book by the Drake School Board in 1973, Vonnegut responded:

> "If you were to bother to read my books, to behave as educated persons would, you would learn that they are not sexy, and do not argue in favor of wildness of any kinds. They beg that people be kinder and more responsible than they often are. It is true that some characters speak coarsely. That is because people speak coarsely in real life. Especially soldiers and hard-working men speak coarsely, and even our most sheltered children know that." (Ziegfeld, Richard E. "Kurt Vonnegut on Censorship and Moral Values."
> *Modern Fiction Studies* 26 [Winter 1980–1981]: 631–35.)

Banned in Levittown, New York (1975); in North Jackson, Ohio (1979); and in Lakeland, Florida (1982), because of the "book's explicit sexual scenes, violence, and obscene language."

Barred from purchase at the Washington Park High School in Racine, Wisconsin (1984), by the district administrative assistant for instructional services.

Challenged at the Owensboro (Ky.) High School Library (1985) because of "foul language, a section depicting a picture of an act of bestiality, a reference to 'Magic Fingers' attached to the protagonist's bed to help him sleep," and the sentence "The gun made a ripping sound like the opening of the fly of God Almighty."

Restricted to students who have parental permission at the four Racine (Wis.) Unified District high school libraries (1986) because of "language used in the book, depictions of torture, ethnic slurs, and negative portrayals of women."

Challenged in the La Rue County (Ky.) High School Library (1987) by parents who objected that the book is "undermining Christian faith, glorifying death, and containing profanity."

Banned from the Fitzgerald (Ga.) schools (1987) because it is "filled with profanity and full of explicit sexual references."

Challenged in the Baton Rouge (La.) public high school libraries (1988) because the book is "vulgar and offensive."

Challenged in the Monroe (Mich.) public schools (1989) as required reading in a modern novel course for high school juniors and seniors because of the book's language and the way women are portrayed.

## Reviews

*American Scholar* 38 (Autumn 1969): 718.

*Atlantic* 223 (April 1969): 145.

*Best Sellers* 29 (April 15, 1969): 31.

*Booklist* 81 (July 1985): 1547.

*Book World* 19 (July 23, 1989): 10.

*Christian Century* 86 (Aug. 13, 1969): 1069.

*Christian Science Monitor* 61 (Aug. 17, 1969): 15.

*Commonweal* 90 (June 6, 1969): 347.

*Library Journal* 94 (March 1, 1969): 1021; 94 (Dec. 15, 1969): 4624.

*Literature and History* 12 (Spring 1986): 53.

*Locus* 32 (June 1994): 60.

*Nation* 208 (June 9, 1969): 736.

*New Republic* 160 (April 26, 1969): 33.

*New York Times Book Review* (April 6, 1969): 1.

*New Yorker* 45 (May 17, 1969): 145.

*Newsweek* 73 (April 14, 1969): 122.

*Saturday Review* 52 (March 29, 1969): 25.

*Time* 93 (April 11, 1969): 106.

## Articles about This Book

Bianculli, David. "A Kurt Post-Mortem on the Generally Eclectic Theater." *Film Comment* 21 (Dec. 1985): 41.

Blackford, R. "Physics and Fantasy: Scientific Mysticism, Kurt Vonnegut, and *Gravity's Rainbow*." *Journal of Popular Culture* 19 (Winter 1985): 35–44.

"Facts Worse than Death." *North American Review* 267 (Dec. 1982): 46–49.

Giannone, R. "Violence in the Fiction of Kurt Vonnegut." *Thought* 56 (March 1981): 58–76.

Gill, R. B. "Bargaining in Good Faith: The Laughter of Vonnegut, Grass, and Dundera." *Critique* 25 (Winter 1984): 77–91.

Hume, K. "Kurt Vonnegut and the Myths and Symbols of Meaning." *Texas Studies in Literature and Language* 24 (Winter 1982): 429–47.

"Hypocrites You Always Have with You." *Nation* 230 (April 19, 1980): 469–70.

Matheson, T. J. "This Lousy Little Book: The Genesis and Development of *Slaughterhouse-Five* as Revealed in Chapter One." *Studies in the Novel* 16 (Summer 1984): 228–40.

"MCLU Survey Finds Censorship in Minnesota 'Appalling.'" *Library Journal* 74 (Feb. 15, 1982): 386.

Musil, Robert K. "There Must Be More to Love than Death: A Conversation with Kurt Vonnegut." *Nation* 231 (Aug. 2, 1980): 128.

Nuwer, H. "Kurt Vonnegut Close Up." *Saturday Evening Post* 258 (May–June 1986): 38–39.

"Reluctant Big Shot." *Nation* 232 (March 7, 1981): 282.

"Truly Modern Hero." *Psychology Today* 15 (Aug. 1981): 9–10.

Veix, Donald B. "Teaching a Censored Novel: *Slaughterhouse-Five*." *English Journal* 64 (Oct. 1975): 25.

"Vonnegut: The Fundamental Piece of Obscenity." *Publishers Weekly* 229 (Jan. 31, 1986): 263.

"War Preparers Anonymous." (Excerpt from address on Jan. 17, 1984.) *Harper's* 268 (March 1984): 41.

Ziegfeld, R. E. "Kurt Vonnegut on Censorship and Moral Values." *Modern Fiction Studies* 26 (Winter 1980–81): 631–35.

## Background

Goldsmith, David H. *Kurt Vonnegut: Fantasist of Fire and Ice.* Bowling Green, Ohio: Bowling Green University Press, 1972.

Jinkowitz, Jerome. *Kurt Vonnegut.* New York: Methuen, 1982.

Lundquist, James. *Kurt Vonnegut.* New York: Ungar, 1977.

Mayo, Clark. *Kurt Vonnegut: The Gospel from Outer Space; or, Yes We Have No Nirvanas.* San Bernardino, Calif.: Borgo Press, 1977.

*The Vonnegut Statement.* Eds. Jerome Klinkowitz and John Somer. New York: Delacorte, 1973.

## Awards and Prizes

Still Alive: The Best of the Best Books for Young Adults, 1975

## References about the Author

*Contemporary Authors, New Revision Series.* Detroit: Gale, 1981. v. 1, pp. 678–84.

*Contemporary Literary Criticism.* Detroit: Gale, dates vary. v. 1, pp. 347–48; v. 2, pp. 451–56; v. 3, pp. 494–506; v. 4, pp. 460–70; v. 5, pp. 464–71; v. 8, pp. 529–35; v. 12, pp. 600–630; v. 22, pp. 444–52.

*Current Biography Yearbook, 1970.* Ed. Charles Moritz. New York: Wilson, 1971. pp. 429–32.

*Dictionary of Literary Biography.* Vol. 8: *Twentieth-Century American Science Fiction Writers, Part 2: M-Z.* Eds. David Cowart and Thomas L. Wymer. Detroit: Gale, 1981. pp. 184–90.

## Sources Recommending This Book

*Fiction Catalog.* 13th ed. Eds. Juliette Yaakov and John Greenfieldt. New York: H. W. Wilson, 1996. p. 677.

*Fiction for Youth: A Guide to Recommended Books.* 2nd ed. Ed. Lillian Shapiro. New York: Neal-Schuman Publishers, 1986. p. 195.

Gillespie, John T., ed. *Best Books for Senior High Readers.* New Providence, N.J.: R. R. Bowker, 1991. p. 66.

*The Reader's Advisor: The Best in Reference Works, British Literature and American Literature.* 14th ed. 3 vols. New York: R. R. Bowker, 1994. v. 1, p. 1063.

*Senior High School Library Catalog.* 14th ed. Eds. Brenda Smith and Juliette Yaakov. New York: H. W. Wilson, 1992. p. 72.

*Top One Hundred Countdown: Best of the Best Books for Young Adults, 1969–1994.* Chicago: American Library Association, 1995.

Young Adult Library Services Association. *Outstanding Books for the College Bound: Choices for a Generation.* Chicago: American Library Association, 1996.

*The Young Adult Reader's Adviser.* Vol. 1, *The Best in Literature and Language Arts, Mathematics, and Computer Science.* Ed. Myra Immell. New Providence, N.J.: R. R. Bowker, 1992. pp. 296–97.

## Audiovisual Resources

*Slaughterhouse-Five.* 12-inch, 33⅓ RPM record. 2 sides. Producer and distributor: Angel Records, 1750 N. Vine St., Los Angeles, CA 90028.

*Slaughterhouse-Five.* 2 x 2 slide, no accompanying material. 90 frames. Producer and distributor: Thomas S. Klise, P.O. Box 3418, Peoria, IL 61614; (309) 676-5311.

*Slaughterhouse-Five.* 1-track, 1⅞ cassette. Producer and distributor: Caedmon Records, 1995 Broadway, New York, NY 10023.

LINDA MADARAS with DANE SAAVEDRA

# The What's Happening to My Body Book for Boys

New York: Newmarket Press, 1984

LINDA MADARAS with AREA MADARAS

# The What's Happening to My Body Book for Girls

New York: Newmarket Press, 1987

Linda Madaras, with the assistance of her daughter (for the girls' book) and a friend's son (for the boys' book), has written gender-specific guides for children approaching or experiencing puberty. Her tone is conversational, nonjudgmental, and generally humorous. Much of the material in these two texts is based on her sex-education classes in a middle school in Pasadena, California.

The books contain information about bodily changes and are geared toward young people between the ages of nine and about sixteen. Sexually transmitted diseases, including AIDS, are discussed at some length. Sexual intercourse is explained and illustrated with drawings. Pregnancy is detailed and birth control is included, but youngsters needing detailed information about birth control must find it elsewhere.

Madaras's discussions are clear and frank, as are the book's line-drawing illustrations. Each book has a chapter about puberty in the opposite sex.

While children want and need the information in Madaras's books, her sections on birth control and masturbation and her tolerant view of homosexuality have created challenges to these books in many libraries.

## Challenges

### The What's Happening to My Body Book for Boys

Challenged at the Mt. Morris (Ill.) School District seventh-grade class (1986) because it is written from a "permissive point of view."

Challenged in the Kenai Peninsula Borough School in Homer, Alaska (1993), because of objection to the way masturbation and homosexuality were presented, as well as two slang words used to describe sexual methods and the male anatomy.

Challenged, but retained, at the Cleveland (Tenn.) Public Library (1993), along with 17 other books, most of which were on sex education and AIDS awareness.

Challenged in 1994, but retained, at the Washoe County Library System, in Reno, Nevada, because "nobody in their right mind would give a book like that to children on their own, except the library."

In 1994, after a parent complained, "I don't think my ten-year-old son or anyone's need to know that stuff," the book was determined missing from the Northside Intermediate School Library in Milton, Wisconsin.

### The What's Happening to My Body Book for Girls

Challenged at the Mt. Morris (Ill.) School District seventh-grade class (1986) because it is written from a "permissive point of view."

Challenged, but retained, at the Cleveland (Tenn.) Public Library (1993), along with 17 other books, most of which were on sex education and AIDS awareness.

## Reviews

### The What's Happening to My Body Book for Boys

*Booklist* 81 (Nov. 15, 1984): 432; 82 (Nov. 15, 1985): 485; 88 (June 1, 1992): 1727; 91 (Oct. 15, 1994): 412.

*Bulletin of the Center for Children's Books* 38 (March 1985): 130.

*Emergency Librarian* 16 (Sept. 1988): 58.

*Journal of Youth Services in Libraries* 8 (Winter 1995): 215.

*Kirkus Reviews* 52 (Sept. 15, 1984): 898.

*Kliatt Paperback Book Guide* 19 (Winter 1985): 43.

*Ms.* 13 (Jan. 1985): 20.

*Parents Magazine* 69 (Aug. 1994): 84.

*Publishers Weekly* 226 (Oct. 5, 1984): 85.

*School Library Journal* 31 (March 1985): 180; 37 (April 1991): 41.

*Voice of Youth Advocates* 8 (June 1985): 146; 12 (June 1989): 126.

*Wilson Library Bulletin* 63 (May 1989): 111.

### The What's Happening to My Body Book for Girls

*Booklist* 91 (Oct. 15, 1994): 412.

*Emergency Librarian* 16 (Sept. 1988): 58.

*Journal of Youth Services in Libraries* 8 (Winter 1995): 215.

*School Library Journal* 37 (April 1991): 41.

*Voice of Youth Advocates* 12 (June 1989): 126.

*Wilson Library Bulletin* 63 (May 1989): 111.

## Sources Recommending This Book

### The What's Happening to My Body Book for Boys

Gillespie, John T., ed. *Best Books for Junior High Readers*. New Providence, N.J.: R. R. Bowker, 1991. p. 205.

*High-Low Handbook: Encouraging Literacy in the 1990s*. 3rd ed. Comp. and ed. Ellen V. LiBretto. New York: R. R. Bowker, 1990. p. 245.

*Top One Hundred Countdown: Best of the Best Books for Young Adults, 1969–1994*. Chicago: American Library Association, 1995.

*The Young Adult Reader's Adviser*. Vol. 2, *The Best in Social Sciences, History, Science, and Health*. Ed. Myra Immell. New Providence, N.J.: R. R. Bowker, 1992. p. 542.

Zvirin, Stephanie, *Best Years of Their Lives: A Resource Guide for Teenagers in Crisis*. 2nd ed. Chicago: American Library Association, 1996. p. 78.

### The What's Happening to My Body Book for Girls

Carter, Betty. *Best Books for Young Adults: The History, the Selections, the Romance*. Chicago: American Library Association, 1994. pp. 122, 164.

Gillespie, John T., ed. *Best Books for Junior High Readers*. New Providence, N.J.: R. R. Bowker, 1991. p. 204.

*High-Low Handbook: Encouraging Literacy in the 1990s*. 3rd ed. Comp. and ed. Ellen V. LiBretto. New York: R. R. Bowker, 1990. p. 246.

*The Young Adult Reader's Adviser*. Vol. 2, *The Best in Social Sciences, History, Science, and Health*. Ed. Myra Immell. New Providence, N.J.: R. R. Bowker, 1992. p. 542.

Zvirin, Stephanie. *Best Years of Their Lives: A Resource Guide for Teenagers in Crisis*. 2nd ed. Chicago: American Library Association, 1996. p. 78.

# What ALA Can Do to Help Librarians Combat Censorship

The American Library Association maintains a broad program for the promotion and defense of intellectual freedom, composed of the Intellectual Freedom Committee; the Office for Intellectual Freedom (OFI); the Intellectual Freedom Round Table; the Intellectual Freedom Action Network; the Freedom to Read Foundation; and the LeRoy C. Merritt Humanitarian Fund.

The basic program of the Intellectual Freedom Committee is educational in nature. The most effective safeguards for the rights of library users and librarians are an informed public and a library profession aware of repressive activities and how to combat them. Toward this end, the administrative arm of the Intellectual Freedom Committee, the Office for Intellectual Freedom, implements ALA policies on intellectual freedom and educates librarians about the importance of the concept. The Office for Intellectual Freedom maintains a wide-ranging program of educational and informational publications, projects, and services.

*The Newsletter on Intellectual Freedom,* the official bimonthly publication of the Intellectual Freedom Committee, was initiated in 1952 and has been edited and produced by the OIF staff since 1970. The *Newsletter* is addressed to both librarians and members of the general public concerned about intellectual freedom. Its main purpose is to provide a comprehensive national picture of censorship efforts, court cases, legislation, and current readings on the subject. Through original and reprinted articles, the *Newsletter* offers a forum for expressing varying views about intellectual freedom, while providing a means for reporting activities of the Intellectual Freedom Committee, the Office for Intellectual Freedom, and the Freedom to Read Foundation. In 1982, noted civil liberties authority Nat Hentoff named the *Newsletter* "the best small publication in America." It is available by subscription from the Office for Intellectual Freedom.

*The Intellectual Freedom Action News* is a different publication: a

---

Adapted in part from the *Intellectual Freedom Manual,* 5th ed., by the Office for Intellectual Freedom (American Library Association, 1996).

brief, informal monthly newsletter designed to provide updates on late-breaking censorship controversies or legislation that could impact intellectual freedom in libraries and to alert members and supporters to areas where they may find additional information or localities where their assistance is needed. *The Action News* serves as the newsletter (both print and electronic) for the Intellectual Freedom Action Network, a grassroots, ad hoc group of volunteers who have identified themselves as willing to come forward in support of the freedom to read in censorship controversies in their communities. It is also circulated to state chapter and divisional intellectual freedom committees, ALA chapter councilors, and others who indicate interest. *The Action News* provides information that may assist network members in the promotion and defense of intellectual freedom, and it gives suggestions for new programs and project ideas.

The Office for Intellectual Freedom also produces and distributes documents, articles, and ALA policies concerning intellectual freedom to both librarians and the general public. Monographs, resource guides, training materials, and manuals include the *Intellectual Freedom Manual*; the annually produced *Banned Books Week Resource Kit; Confidentiality in Libraries: An Intellectual Freedom Modular Education Program*; and *Censorship and Selection: Issues and Answers for Schools* (Revised edition by Henry Reichman). During nationwide controversies concerning individual titles, press clippings, editorials, and public statements detailing the ways various libraries around the country handled requests to remove specific materials are compiled and sent out to others handling similar problems.

One of the most often used and least heard about functions of the Office is its provision of advice and consultation (case support) to individuals involved in potential or actual censorship controversies. Rarely does a day go by without a request by phone or letter asking for advice about a specific book, video, or audio recording that has drawn the censorious attention of an individual or group. When contacted for assistance, the Office provides reviews and information about the author of the challenged material, applicable ALA policies, advice about the implementation of reconsideration policies, and other counseling specific to the situation at hand. Or, if requested, the Office can provide the names of persons available to offer testimony or support before library boards, supplied from the ranks of the Intellectual Freedom Action Network and state library association intellectual freedom committees. The options chosen are always the prerogative of the individual requesting assistance. If a censorship problem arises, librarians should contact the Office for Intellectual Freedom (50 East Huron Street, Chicago, IL 60611; (312) 280-4223 or (800) 545-2433, extension 4223).

In 1990, the Office for Intellectual Freedom established a censorship database to record and report statistics on challenges to library materials across the country. The database is a useful tool for identifying trends in types of censorship cases and for documenting responses and solutions to these cases. All librarians are encouraged to document and report challenges—and their outcome—to the Office for Intellectual Freedom. Information about the particular institution, its specific locations, and the parties involved are kept confidential until—and only if—the information is published elsewhere. For statistical purposes, and to inform the public of the prevalence of censorship problems in our society, the Office might release only the name of the challenged material and the state in which the challenge occurred.

The Office for Intellectual Freedom welcomes reports in the form of newspaper clippings, magazine articles, cards, and letters.

Of special importance to individuals facing challenges are state library association intellectual freedom committees. The extent and nature of the activities of these committees vary from state to state. Some groups are more active than others. In some states, the committees have worked with other organizations to build impressive state coalitions in defense of intellectual and academic freedom. Elsewhere they have concentrated on compiling and developing state intellectual freedom manuals and continuing education materials. The relationship of the ALA Intellectual Freedom Committee and the Office with the state committees is one of mutual cooperation and assistance. The Office supports the work at the state level with information, coordination, and ideas. On their part, the state committees can be the Office's "eyes and ears" at the local level.

## Online Resources

With the increased use of the Internet for communicating, the Office for Intellectual Freedom established a "listserv" to allow discussion among persons interested in the issue of intellectual freedom. An unmoderated list, ALAOIF is among the most popular lists currently available.

To subscribe, send the message "subscribe alaoif <your first name> <your last name>" to listproc@ala.org.

The *Library Bill of Rights,* along with other American Library Association intellectual freedom policies, can be found on the ALA Home Page at http://www.ala.org.

## Banned Books Week

The event that draws the most attention to the Office for Intellectual Freedom is the yearly celebration, Banned Books Week—Celebrating the

Freedom to Read. Banned Books Week began in 1982 to call attention to the danger of censorship and encourage support for the freedom to read. It is sponsored by the American Library Association and cosponsored by the American Booksellers Association, the American Booksellers Foundation for Free Expression, the Association of American Publishers, the American Society of Journalists and Authors, and the National Association of College Stores. It is also endorsed by the Center for the Book of the Library of Congress.

Each year, in conjunction with Banned Books Week, OIF releases a *Resource Guide* for use by libraries, bookstores, and other organizations. It includes a list of books that have been banned or challenged during the previous year.

The challenges included in the report represent only those that have been reported publicly. No names of parents or others registering complaints are published.

Becoming involved and working together with colleagues and friends, librarians can fulfill their mission to confront censorship and protect access to the broadest range of information.